Country
Walks
Near
Baltimore

ALSO PUBLISHED BY THE
APPALACHIAN MOUNTAIN CLUB

Country Walks Near Washington
Alan Fisher

Southern Snow
The Winter Guide to Dixie
Randy Johnson

Hiking the Mountain State
The Trails of West Virginia
Allen de Hart

North Carolina Hiking Trails
Allen de Hart

Whitewater Handbook
John Urban
Revised by T. Walley Williams

River Rescue
Les Bechdel and Slim Ray

Mountain Passages
An Appalachia Anthology
Edited by Robert E. Manning

Moving Mountains
Coping with Change in Mountain Communities
Sara Neustadtl
Foreword by Arlene Blum

Country Walks Near Baltimore

Second Edition

by Alan Fisher

APPALACHIAN MOUNTAIN CLUB
BOSTON, MASSACHUSETTS

Library of Congress Cataloging-in-Publication Data

Fisher, Alan (Alan Hall)
　　Country walks near Baltimore/by Alan Fisher.—2nd ed.
　　　　p.　cm.
　　Bibliography: p.
　　ISBN 0-910146-66-7 (alk. paper)
　　　1. Walking—Maryland—Baltimore Region—Guide–books.　2. Baltimore
　Region (Md.)—Description and travel—Guide–books.　I. Appalachian
　Mountain Club.　II. Title.　III. Title: Country walks near Baltimore.
　IV. Title: Country walks near Baltimore.
　GV199.42.M32B343 1988　　　　　　　　　　　　　　87-31843
　917.52'60443—dc19　　　　　　　　　　　　　　　　　CIP

SECOND EDITION

The paper used in this publication meets the minimum requirements
of the American National Standard for Information Sciences—Permanence of Paper for Printed Library Materials, ANSI Z39.48-
1984.♾™

**Due to changes in conditions, use of the information in this book
is at the sole risk of the user.**

Printed in the United States of America

10　9　8　7　6　5　4　3　2　　　　　　　88　89　90　91　92

CONTENTS

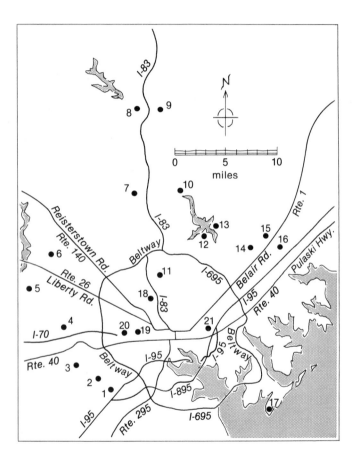

PREFACE

THERE'S STILL TIME for a walk in the woods, even if you've spent all morning working or sleeping late.

This book is for people who want an outing in the country without wasting half the day getting there and back. If you live in the Baltimore area, the excursions described here are close at hand. Some are near bus lines; all are easily reached by car. The walks have been planned to show the best parts of Baltimore's countryside and to encourage everyone to use the many large parks and extensive trail networks maintained by state, county, and city agencies, and private conservation groups.

Each chapter of this book includes a brief introduction, a map, directions, and commentary on the area's natural or social history or other pertinent issues. The maps, directions, and commentary have all been reviewed and updated for this 2nd edition. Also, a new chapter (Chapter 10—the Northern Central Railroad Trail) has been added. The routes cover the gamut of Maryland's Piedmont and Coastal Plain landscapes: steep-sided river valleys, farmland, rolling hills, rocky barrens, flood plain, marsh, and shore, as well as historic houses, mill sites, and ruins along the way. All the areas included here are open to the public, and many are excellent for ski touring as well as walking. The excursions are attractive at all times of the year, and successive visits during different seasons provide added enjoyment.

A few comments on how to dress and what to bring may be in order. Wear shoes that you do not mind getting muddy or wet. Sneakers or running shoes are adequate in warm weather; hiking shoes or boots are advisable during winter. I usually carry a small knapsack containing lunch, a plastic water bottle, perhaps a sweater or rain parka, and some insect repellent during summer. To help keep the trails free from drooping branches, you may also want to bring a small pair of pruning shears.

It is customary in books such as this to include a catalog of cautions about poison ivy, slippery rocks, and the like. Such a list follows, but more generally, of course, what is needed is simply common sense. Each year thousands of people walk the trails described here without injury, but there are always those who are hurt or even killed because they fail to take ordinary care or willfully take extraordinary risks. Specifically, during winter do not walk on frozen rivers, ponds, or lakes. Do not go swimming except where and when permitted. Even wading can be dangerous because of strong currents, so where the routes described here ford streams, do not cross if the water is more than ankle deep. Stay back from the edges of cliffs, and keep in mind that terrain presenting only moderate difficulty when dry can be treacherous when wet or icy. In sum, use good judgment and common sense to evaluate the particular circumstances that you find and do not undertake any unusual risks.

A few of the routes described here follow roads for short distances. In such cases, walk on the road's left shoulder—or altogether off the road, if possible—in order to minimize the risk of being hit by a car approaching from behind. Use caution, especially at dusk or after dark, where the routes cross roads and railroads. (Studies show that in poor light conditions, motorists cannot even see pedestrians in time to stop, so your safety depends entirely upon you.) Also, because some of these walks are in urban parks, it is unwise to go alone or after dark.

Every year the newspapers carry stories about people who pick up a squirrel, a raccoon, or some other animal and get bitten. They then have to undergo a series of painful anti-rabies shots. Don't be one of these people; don't handle *any* animals. In somewhat the same vein, remember that the Baltimore region is inhabited by poisonous copperhead snakes. Be careful where you place your hands and feet, particularly in rocky areas. On a more mundane level, during spring and summer check your clothing and body for ticks after your walk.

As noted in the directions toward the end of each chapter, some of the walks described here are easily reached by the buses of the Mass Transit Administration. If you plan to take an MTA bus, always call 539–5000 beforehand to check on the route, schedule, and connecting buses for the trip both out and back. Specify the day that you are thinking of going; bus schedules and routes are frequently different for weekdays, Saturday, and Sunday.

If you are going by car, it is anticipated that for some of the areas discussed here, readers will be approaching from different directions; accordingly, the instructions sometimes outline several different avenues of approach. Read through the automobile directions before you start in order to pinpoint your destination and to pick the best way to get there.

Finally, I want to say a few words about trash. Dumping is a problem that plagues our state and local parks. Some businesses appear to make regular use of the parks to dispose of their used tires, rubbish, construction rubble, or whatever. If you see someone dumping refuse, note the license number, model, and color of the vehicle and a description of the person, then report the incident to the police and also to the agency that manages the park (listed in the introduction to each chapter). Urge the park agencies to construct and maintain effective barriers to prevent dumpers from driving into the woods on park trails. As for litter such as beer cans and pop bottles, please pick up what you can.

I have received information and other help for this revised edition from the following people: Frazier Bishop, Frank Bolton, Edward S. Corbett, Brent Hartley, William O. Johnson, Jody Landers, Harry J. McCullough, John W. McGrain, Joseph L. Mullen, Tolly Peuleché, Judith Plott, William H. Riley III, Rudolph Rivers, Jody Roesler, Peggy Ross, Charles Van-

Scoit, Robert W. Stanhope, Marilyn Walker, John Wilson, and Peggy Wilson. Many, many thanks.

Alan Fisher
Baltimore

1

PATAPSCO VALLEY STATE PARK

Avalon and Orange Grove

Walking and ski touring—4.0 miles (6.4 kilometers). From the Avalon area (shown on the cover of this book) follow River Road upstream along the southwest bank of the Patapsco River. Cross the swinging bridge at Orange Grove, then return downstream on a wide path along the northeast bank. River Road is closed to cars on Friday, Saturday, Sunday, and state holidays; however, in order to cross back over the river at Avalon, the last 0.5 mile of the circuit follows park roads that remain open to automobile traffic, so in this area, extra caution is necessary. As shown on the map, several footpaths also follow the side of the valley above River Road. If you are looking for a country setting in which to push your child in a stroller, River Road makes an excellent promenade during the period that it is closed to cars. The park opens daily at 10 AM during the colder months and at 8 AM during the warmer months. Year-round, the park closes at sunset. It is also closed on Christmas. An admission fee is charged on weekends during March through October. Dogs are prohibited. Managed by the Maryland Park Service (telephone 461–5005).

BETWEEN WOODSTOCK (west of Baltimore) and tidewater at Elkridge, the Patapsco River falls more than 200 feet in a distance of 17 miles, much of it through a steep-sided valley. The potential of this stretch of river for water power was not lost on the ironmongers, millers, textile manufacturers,

and other early industrialists of the eighteenth and nineteenth centuries, and during that period many dams and factories were built in the narrow valley, notably at Elysville (now Daniels), Ellicotts Upper and Lower Mills, Oella, Ilchester, Orange Grove, and Avalon. This and the following three walks pass these sites. A few are still active mills; others are just ruins or stretches of wooded valley where whole factory villages have been obliterated by fire and flood and whose names survive only as designations for different sections of the Patapsco Valley State Park.

Avalon is one of these lost towns. It got its start in the 1760s when Caleb Dorsey, ironmaster and owner of Elkridge Furnace, built a forge upstream from his furnace for fashioning implements from the pig iron that he produced. According to the nineteenth-century memoirs of Martha Ellicott Tyson (a descendant of the Ellicotts of Ellicott City), the only iron tools made in Baltimore County prior to the American Revolution were crowbars produced at Dorsey's Forge. All other tools were imported, as was intended under the British mercantile system by which the colonies were to provide raw materials—including pig iron—to England and to purchase finished goods in return.

During the Revolution, a mill to produce rolled, slit, and sheet iron was established at Avalon by William Whitcroft of Annapolis, who had received a government loan voted by the Convention, Maryland's revolutionary legislature. By 1777 Whitcroft's Patapsco Slitting Mill was producing nails. This was the first nail factory in Maryland; apparently it was quite primitive, since the individual nails had to be headed one at a time by hand. Whitcroft's lease with Caleb Dorsey's son Edward (known as Iron Head Ned) stipulated that Dorsey would raise his forge dam at Avalon an additional foot and dig a race to Whitcroft's mill for water power to run the bellows and other machinery; in exchange, Whitcroft would not only pay rent for use of the site but would also buy all of his raw iron from Edward Dorsey, who later purchased the Whitcroft mill for himself.

8

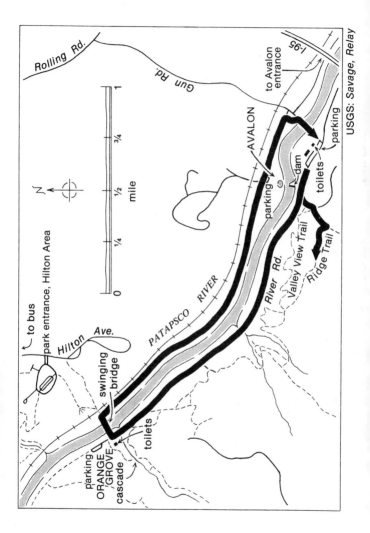

USGS: *Savage, Relay*

After Edward Dorsey's death in 1815, the forge and slitting mill were purchased at auction by two members of the enterprising Ellicott family, who then rebuilt the old works. By 1820 the Ellicott iron works—one at Avalon (the name was first used by the Ellicotts) and another a few miles upstream at Ellicott City—were listed together in the census as having between them four rolling mills, six pairs of rollers with the necessary furnaces, and twenty-four nail machines. Fifty men and thirteen boys were employed to produce nails, barrel hoops, and iron rods.

During the next half-century, the Avalon nail factory was sold and expanded a number of times. After being pulled down and rebuilt on a larger scale in the early 1850s, the factory reached its peak in about 1856, producing 44,000 kegs of nails from forty-four machines. In a panoramic print of Avalon in 1857, the iron works are shown as two long buildings resembling train sheds side by side, standing parallel with the river on the east bank near the present-day park bridge. The roofs were supported on brick piers. Four tall smoke stacks rose between the mill sheds, one of which bore a sign saying "Rolling Mill 1855" and the other a sign saying "Puddling Mill Built 1853." Around the factory was a small village, including a church, a school, stores, and about thirty mill houses.

In the following years, however, nail manufacturing at Avalon was reduced due to lack of demand, and by 1864, when the property was sold again, the advertisements stated that the works were used solely as a rolling mill for plate iron. Four years later, on July 24, 1868, the entire factory complex was destroyed in a flood.

There appear to be no contemporary accounts of what happened at Avalon that morning, but the events at nearby Ellicott City, as recalled by Charles F. Kreh who was there at the time, give some idea:

> At about 9:15 o'clock the mail train from Baltimore arrived, and at that hour there was little evidence or intimation of impending disaster in the Patapsco. Only a lowering of the clouds and an unusual darkness, together with some fierce bolts of lightning, ap-

peared to cast their shadows before them and to indicate the coming of a storm. But, as yet, few if any had thought of what was in store for them. Soon, however, came reports of terrible cloudbursts in various places west of the Ellicotts. The Baltimore train left the station and had only reached Union Mills about a mile distant, when it was met by an avalanche of water. The bounds of the river were already broken and only the weight of the train held it to the tracks. Fortunately for the passengers, it stood close by the mountain side, and they were thus enabled to clamber up and return to the city.

Hardly had a few minutes elapsed before the mad waters (in all their intensity and fury and without any warning) burst upon the good people of Ellicotts living along the river course on the Baltimore County side, and almost in a twinkling their homes were surrounded and all avenues of escape cut off. Then began scenes that almost beggar description, many of them pitiful and heartrending. The waters, filled with logs and trees and debris of all kinds, arose as if by magic and seemed to gloat in their power of fierce destruction. Opposite the railroad station across the Patapsco stood a row of houses, some brick, some frame and others stone, extending over a space of about 1000 feet from the bridge to the mill structure . . . and in a remarkably short time these were seen to begin to crumble from the beating of the waves against them. Now could be seen the dwellers breaking through the roofs from house to house and barely escaping the collapse of their homes. The last house in the row was a brick building owned by William Partridge and in this, thirty-odd persons sought refuge. Many were the prayers that went up to the Most High from those looking on from the opposite shore that this house might be spared, but it was not to be, and soon all were engulfed and swallowed up in the angry waters. School children, who had come across the river in the early morning, stood on the banks and saw their parents go to their watery graves.

The flood crest reached 40 feet above normal. At Ellicott City thirty-two buildings were destroyed. Workers fled the factories as the riverside industries were inundated. The massive Granite Cotton Mill in Ellicott City collapsed into the torrent, taking with it one man who had been too slow to leave. Bodies from Ellicott City were recovered near Baltimore, 12 miles downstream. Those of one man and his wife and child were found caught in the top of a tree. In all, about fifty people drowned that morning in the Patapsco Valley.

At Avalon no lives were lost but the factory was wrecked. In testimony from a lawsuit in 1870, the president of The Avalon Nail and Iron Company recalled that nearly all of the machinery was destroyed: "There might have been two or three of the nail machines left, but all of the machinery was broken by the debris which came down." The wreckage was sold for scrap iron. By the turn of the century, even most of the tenant dwellings had vanished. Today only two stone houses survive, of which the more conspicuous is located on high ground near the railroad crossing above the park bridge.

Since 1868 the Patapsco Valley has experienced lesser floods (as it always had) on a more or less regular basis. Tropical Storm Agnes in 1972, however, was of a different order of magnitude: it was comparable to the flood a century earlier. Beginning June 21, the storm lumbered across Maryland in three days of almost constant rain. At Ellicott City, one of the early Ellicott houses that had survived the prior flood was toppled. Over $1,800,000 in damage occurred in the Patapsco Valley State Park alone. At Avalon, the high water washed out the east end of the dam over which the river used to flow. The park bridge was destroyed, as were most other small bridges. Shelters were swept away and the swinging footbridge at Orange Grove was pulled down. Between Ilchester and Avalon the current ate away long stretches of River Road and the B&O railbed, and the large sanitary sewer that runs down the valley was ruptured in four places.

Since 1972 much of the damage has been repaired. The swinging bridge has been replaced and River Road has been reconstructed between Avalon and Orange Grove. New restrooms and picnic shelters have been constructed. For infomation about the use of these shelters, call the park office.

BUS: As shown on the map and reflected in the Automobile and Walk directions, the excursion starts at the Avalon sec-

tion of the Patapsco Valley State Park. However, if you are going by bus, the best approach is via the Hilton Avenue entrance shown at the top of the map. This approach involves an extra 1.5 miles of walking each way between the bus stop in Catonsville and the Hilton Avenue entrance, but (after all) walking is what this book is about, and this section of the Patapsco Valley is very attractive.

From downtown Baltimore, take the MTA Catonsville bus (#2) west via Fayette Street and Frederick Avenue/Road through Catonsville. Get off where Rolling Road intersects Frederick Road from the south (or left) opposite Hillcrest Elementary School. You will know that your stop is coming after the bus passes over the Beltway and through the Catonsville business district.

From the bus stop, walk south on Rolling Road about 200 yards, then continue straight on Hilton Avenue where Rolling Road veers left. Follow Hilton Avenue 1.5 miles to the Patapsco Valley State Park entrance on the right. Where there is no sidewalk, be alert for cars; walk on the road's left shoulder to minimize the risk of being hit by a car approaching from behind.

With your back to the small ranger station at the park entrance, follow the circle road left (or clockwise) one quarter of the way around the loop to an intersection with a road leading right to a parking lot. About 20 yards beyond this intersection, a wide dirt path leaves the outer edge of the loop past two wooden posts. Follow the path downhill for several hundred yards past picnic sites and through the woods to an overlook above the river and railroad tracks. With caution, descend very steeply to the left. After checking for oncoming trains, cross the tracks; if a train on the siding blocks the way, detour to the right 200 yards around the end of the siding, but allow ample leeway in case the train starts to move. After crossing the tracks, descend to the riverside path and the swinging footbridge, where you can pick up the circuit shown on the map.

AUTOMOBILE: The section of the Patapsco Valley State Park explored by this walk is located southwest of Baltimore. The entrance is off South Street near its intersection with Route 1 (Washington Boulevard) 0.2 mile northeast of the Patapsco River.

From Baltimore, take Interstate 95 south toward Washington. Interstate 95 southbound can also be reached from exit 11B off Interstate 695 (the Beltway). Follow Interstate 95 about 1.7 miles southwest of the Beltway, then take exit 47B-A for Route 166 and Catonsville, but immediately fork left for exit 47A and Route 166 south toward U.S. Route 1. Follow Route 166 for 0.8 mile, then take the exit for Route 1 south toward Washington. Bear right onto Route 1, then immediately turn right again onto South Street. Go only 100 yards, then turn left into the entrance for Patapsco Valley State Park—Avalon Area.

Follow the entrance road 1.2 miles, past a small ranger station and under both the stone-arch Thomas Viaduct and the high Interstate 95 bridge. At a T-intersection, turn left. Cross the Patapsco River and turn right into the large Avalon parking lot.

WALK: With the Patapsco River toward your right, follow a road that starts at the end of the parking lot and leads 1.6 miles to the swinging bridge at Orange Grove. The road is closed to motor vehicles on Friday, Saturday, Sunday, and state holidays, but the wisest policy is always to be alert for cars.

With the river toward your right, follow the road to the swinging bridge. Or, if you want, take one of the more strenuous footpaths that start just upstream from the old Avalon dam and follow the side and rim of the valley, as shown on the map. The main alternative to the riverside road is the Ridge Trail, blazed with red-orange paint and starting as a gravel road 100 yards upstream from the dam.

At the swinging bridge, a spur trail marked with blue

blazes starts at some stone steps located a few yards up-stream from the bridge. This trail leads 25 yards uphill and along the side of a ravine to an attractive cascade.

To return from Orange Grove to the Avalon parking lot, cross the Patapsco River on the swinging bridge, then turn right. With the river on your right, follow the path down-stream. After 1.5 miles, you will reach a parking lot next to a pond. Continue straight along the road, but be alert for cars. During park hours, this road is open to motor ve-hicles, so walk on the far left in order to minimize the risk of being hit by a car approaching from behind. With cau-tion, follow the road 0.3 mile, then turn right just before a road junction, where the factory village of Avalon was for-merly located. Cross an old stone bridge over a ditch, then cross the Patapsco River on an automobile bridge. Return to your starting point at the large parking lot.

2

PATAPSCO VALLEY STATE PARK

Orange Grove and Ilchester

Walking—4.5 miles (7.2 kilometers). From the park's Hilton entrance, follow a rugged trail that threads through a deep ravine, then climbs along a ridge above the Patapsco River. Continue on Hilltop Road (be alert for cars) to the old but still active mill at Ilchester. Return on a riverside path past the Bloede Dam to the cascade, swinging bridge, and ruins at Orange Grove. Although—or perhaps because—part of the route follows local roads for about a mile, this excursion provides a fascinating and unprettified glimpse of a factory hamlet typical of the mill villages that used to be nestled at intervals in the Patapsco Valley. The park opens daily at 10 AM during the colder months and at 8 AM during the warmer months. Year-round, the park closes at sunset. It is also closed on Christmas. An admission fee is charged on weekends during March through October. Dogs are prohibited. Managed by the Maryland Park Service (telephone 461–5005).

THE MASSIVE STONE WALL shown on the facing page is situated on the bank of the Patapsco River at Orange Grove. It was once part of the C. A. Gambrill Manufacturing Company's Mill C, which in 1900, was called the largest flour mill east of Minneapolis.

The dam, mill, and village at Orange Grove were located in the narrow valley bottom below the present-day entrance to the state park off Hilton Avenue. According to the memoirs of a

former Orange Grove resident—Thomas LeRoy Phillips, whose father was superintendent of the mill from 1891 to 1904—"the subdued rumble of the mill was heard from early Monday morning to late Saturday evening; the muffled roar of water pouring over the high wooden dam was unbroken; and long freight trains rolled by day and night." The mill was powered by three horizontal water wheels and a Corliss steam engine (of which the day engineer was so fond that he named his son Corliss). Two of its better known brands of flour were Orange Grove and Patapsco Superlative Patent.

A flour mill was first constructed at Orange Grove in 1856, when George Worthington and George Bayly bought land there on both sides of the river. According to the deed, the property included parts of tracts known as "Talbot's Last Shift," "Small Bit," "Joseph and Jacob's Invention," and all of "Vortex." It is thought that the new mill and small mill village became known as Orange Grove due to the Osage-orange trees that were common in the area. In 1860 Worthington and Bayly sold the entire property to the C. A. Gambrill Manufacturing Company, which had also taken over the Ellicott family's mill farther upstream. In 1882 the Gambrill Company, trading under the name of Patapsco Flouring Mills, opened a third mill in Baltimore and gave letter designations to the three plants. The one at Ellicott City was Mill A, the Baltimore plant was Mill B, and Orange Grove was Mill C.

In 1875 Gambrill added the Corliss steam engine and boilers to supplement water power at Orange Grove. Eight years later the millstones were replaced by modern steel rollers. The mill building measured 150 by 175 feet. By 1900 it had six stories, four of brick topped by two more of frame and metal siding. A massive rectangular grain elevator 100 by 150 feet and eight stories high flanked the mill on its upstream side, and on the downstream side there was a tall, tapering, square smokestack and a three-story structure housing the Corliss engine, coal bins, and a dynamo that generated electricity to light the mill and the nearby superintendent's house.

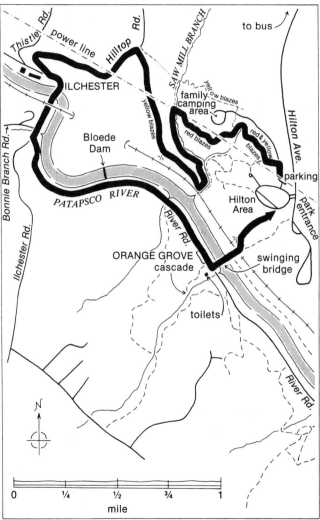

USGS: *Ellicott City, Baltimore West, Savage, Relay*

The entire mill complex was crowded onto a shelf of land between the railroad and a high retaining wall along the river. There was so little room to spare that the former Gun Road (now the riverside path) used to pass through the building in an arched passageway. Trains unloaded grain and coal and picked up flour at the third floor level, since the mill and elevator were set into the hillside. A wooden dam about ten feet high and slightly curved against the pressure of the impounded water created a millpond stretching upstream as far as Ilchester.

On the opposite bank from the mill, a small company-owned village of at least seven houses, a one-room school, and a church was strung out along the river where a parking lot and restrooms are now located. Then, as now, the river was spanned by a swinging bridge, which was snagged and pulled down by an ice jam in January 1904, and again washed out by Tropical Storm Agnes in 1972. A hand pump provided water for the community. Itinerant grocers and butchers with horse-drawn carts supplied some food; other shopping entailed a short train ride to Ellicott City or to Baltimore on one of the twelve passenger trains that stopped daily at Orange Grove. On every third Sunday church services were conducted by a traveling reverend who also preached at Elkridge and at Locust Chapel near Ilchester.

The mill at Orange Grove operated until May 1, 1905, when it was gutted by fire. The remains of the brick walls were torn down, but the dam abutment and large sections of the stone foundations still remain and are passed by the route described below.

BUS: Going by bus involves an extra 1.5 miles of walking each way between the bus stop in Catonsville and the Hilton Avenue entrance to the Patapsco Valley State Park, but the extra effort is worthwhile if the alternative is not going at all.

From downtown Baltimore, take the MTA Catonsville bus (#2) west via Fayette Street and Frederick Avenue/Road through Catonsville. Get off where Rolling Road in-

tersects Frederick Road from the south (or left) opposite Hillcrest Elementary School. You will know that your stop is coming after the bus passes over the Beltway and through the Catonsville business district.

From the bus stop, walk south on Rolling Road about 200 yards, then continue straight on Hilton Avenue where Rolling Road veers left. Follow Hilton Avenue 1.5 miles to the Patapsco Valley State Park entrance on the right. Where there is no sidewalk, be alert for cars; walk on the road's left shoulder to minimize the risk of being hit by a car approaching from behind.

Enter the Hilton Area and pass the small ranger station. Bear right onto a loop road, then turn right again at the first intersection toward the family camping area. Follow the road only a few dozen yards to a large parking lot under high electric transmission lines.

AUTOMOBILE: The section of the Patapsco Valley State Park explored by this walk is located southwest of Baltimore. The entrance is off Hilton Avenue south of Catonsville.

From Interstate 695 (the Beltway) west of Baltimore, take exit 13 for Route 144 (Frederick Road) toward Catonsville. Follow Frederick Road west about 1.1 miles through Catonsville. Turn left where Rolling Road intersects Frederick Road from the south opposite Hillcrest Elementary School. Follow Rolling Road south only 200 yards. Where Rolling Road veers left, continue straight on Hilton Avenue 1.5 miles to the entrance for the Patapsco Valley State Park on the right, 100 yards after the park maintenance complex. Enter the Hilton Area and pass the small ranger station. Bear right onto the loop road, then turn right again at the first opportunity toward the family camping area. Go a few dozen yards to a large parking lot under high electric transmission lines.

WALK: Relative to the way that you first entered the parking lot, the walk starts near the left end of the lot. With caution, follow an asphalt road 65 yards to a broad foot-path on the left marked with red blazes (the Saw Mill Branch Trail). Follow the wide path downhill 125 yards to an intersection on the right with a narrow footpath marked with red and yellow blazes; turn right here. Follow the red and yellow blazes through the woods, occasionally bypass-ing fallen trees. Although the path itself is sometimes ob-scure, the red and yellow blazes lead the way.

After crossing some cobbles and some rivulets that flow left toward the head of a small ravine, the trail turns left. Then, after about 40 yards, the trail splits. Continue straight, following the red blazes downhill. (The yellow-blazed trail curves sharply to the right uphill.)

Follow the narrow, red-blazed trail as it dips and climbs through the woods. Again, the path is sometimes obscure, but the red blazes lead the way. Cross a right-of-way under some power lines. Continue through the woods as the red-blazed footpath curves right and runs more or less parallel with the power lines, which are sometimes visible about 100 yards to the right. Eventually, descend steeply into the valley of Saw Mill Branch. Toward the bottom of the slope, the trail is located directly under the power lines.

At Saw Mill Branch, ford the stream—if the water is not more than ankle deep; if it is deeper, do not try to cross. Climb 10 yards up the opposite bank, then turn left. With Saw Mill Branch on your left, follow the trail downstream. At some places, the streambank and trail are obviously in the process of being undermined by erosion; in these areas, stay back at least 10 yards from the edge, even though the trail appears to follow the brink.

Continue downstream. Although the trail is sometimes very obscure, you cannot get lost; simply follow Saw Mill Branch, keeping the stream on your left. At times, the trail is several dozen yards from the stream; at other times the path is adjacent to the stream; and sometimes the trail even follows the streambed. Eventually, the trail terminates at a railroad.

Facing the railroad, turn around and slowly re-enter the woods about 10 yards, looking for a rough, yellow-blazed footpath that climbs very steeply to the left over rocks and roots. Follow the yellow-blazed trail steeply uphill, with the Patapsco Valley on your left and the deep ravine of Saw Mill Branch on your right. About 175 yards after the path levels off, a rock outcrop on the left provides a particularly good view of the Patapsco Valley, the Bloede Dam, and the road along the opposite bank by which you will return.

Continue on the yellow-blazed path. Pass under the power lines and continue through the woods to Hilltop Road. Follow Hilltop Road to the left, walking on the far left in order to minimize the risk of being hit by a car approaching from behind. (Sorry about the trash; what's your solution?)

Follow Hilltop Road under the power lines. Continue past houses, then steeply downhill. Turn sharply left downhill past stone houses overlooking an industrial complex.

This is Ilchester: a dam, a paper mill, and a few stone mill houses up the hill. In 1837 George and William Morris, two Scottish brothers, established their Thistle Mills here for making cotton print. Thistle Road still links Frederick Road with the river just beyond the upstream end of the mill complex. By 1900 the mill had been converted to spinning silk before being reconverted for the manufacture of cotton duck and tire fabric. Then in 1922 the Bartgis brothers of Baltimore moved their paper carton business into the old Thistle plant, which has since passed through several more hands. The factory now recycles wastepaper to produce paper board, the kind of cardboard used in cereal boxes.

At the bottom of the valley, bear left onto River Road and follow it across the river and under the railroad. Again, be alert for cars. Continue 200 yards beyond the railroad, then turn left onto a barricaded road a few dozen yards beyond the intersection with Bonnie Branch Road.

This section of River Road was washed away by the flood during Tropical Storm Agnes in 1972. The stone arch and abutment at the river's edge are the remains of the B&O Patterson Viaduct, destroyed by the flood of 1868.

With the river on your left, head downstream on the remains of the road. When it disappears (as it does in some places), follow the rough footpath along the river. Continue to the Bloede Dam, built in 1907. Generators were formerly housed in rooms within the dam, which was abandoned in 1927. Under no circumstances should you enter the dam.

With the river on your left, follow the remains of River Road downstream to the swinging bridge, where the village of Orange Grove was located. A few yards upstream from the bridge, a spur trail marked with blue blazes starts at some stone steps and leads 250 yards uphill and along the side of a ravine to an attractive cascade.

From the middle of the swinging bridge, the stone abutment of the old wooden Orange Grove dam is visible (during the leafless season) about 100 yards upstream on the west bank of the river. On the east bank, the stone foundations of the former mill and grain elevator stretch upstream 75 yards along the railroad embankment. The walls are obscured by trees and are best examined close up.

Cross the swinging footbridge and climb straight up the railroad embankment. With caution, cross the railroad. If the way is blocked by a train on the siding, detour 200 yards upstream around the end of the siding and back along the foot of the bluff, allowing ample leeway in case the train starts to move.

After crossing the railroad, climb very steeply half-left up an eroded slope past concrete foundations for stairs that no longer exist. (If you do not like the prospect of climbing this slope, see the next paragraph.) At the crest of the steep bluff, continue straight away from the valley on a path that climbs gradually to the loop road at the Hilton Area. Follow the road left to return to the starting point. Be alert for cars.

If you do not like the prospect of climbing the steep, eroded slope above the railroad, a ravine just to the right provides a more gradual ascent. The path there is obscure and rough, but it leads eventually to Hilton Avenue about 150 yards downhill from the park entrance.

3

ELLICOTT CITY AND OELLA

Walking—1.5 miles (2.4 kilometers). This walk weaves through Ellicott City's steep, narrow streets, passing old granite and clapboard structures that now house a host of interesting specialty shops. The route also passes the B&O Railroad Station Museum (461–1944); telephone for information regarding the museum's hours and admission fees. Near Ellicott City is Oella, a self-contained mill community that is well worth touring by car.

$\mathbf{A}$S A NAME AND ANACHRONISM, Ellicott "City" is on a par with Baltimore "Town" (as colonial Baltimore was known). The Ellicott City charter was revoked, in fact, by the General Assembly in 1935, after a half-century of economic decline in the Patapsco Valley caused by the advent of steam engines as an alternative to water power. Subject to periodic flooding, the valley setting lost its luster. Over a period of decades many old mills were allowed to slip into obsolescence until they were eventually abandoned following some disaster or other.

Today, despite a glossy new varnish of antique chic, Ellicott City retains much of the flavor of the mill town, quarries, and early railroad terminus of its origin. Its stone and frame buildings are jammed along a narrow valley where Frederick Road crosses the river. A mile upstream on the opposite bank is the industrial village of Oella, a remarkable concentration of nineteenth-century mill housing.

In 1772 Joseph, Andrew, and John Ellicott, Quaker brothers from Bucks County, Pennsylvania, bought land on both sides

of the Patapsco River above and below the present site of Ellicott City. Their newly-acquired stretch of valley was uninhabited, uncultivated, and inaccessible except by footpath. The attraction lay in the steep gradient of the river, for the Ellicotts' purchase included the right to impound water for power. In 1774 the brothers also purchased an existing dam and mill for grinding corn four miles upstream, where the river was crossed by the then Frederick Road (now *Old* Frederick Road), at that time a horsepath for pack animals.

Prior to their purchases in the Patapsco Valley, Andrew and John Ellicott had traveled on horseback over the middle counties of Maryland between the Patapsco and the Blue Ridge. They had concluded from their tour of inspection that the region was suited for growing wheat and had ample water power for grinding grain. Tobacco was then the exclusive cash crop near Baltimore, but the European demand for American tobacco had slumped, payment from European dealers was slow, and yields were declining as the soil became depleted. Also, as a matter of agricultural heritage, the new German settlers in central Maryland (where Frederick had been named for the kings of Prussia) preferred to grow wheat. In consequence, the Ellicotts perceived that a regional grain market was in the making. Between 1749 and 1774 the export of wheat and flour from Annapolis had already increased by nearly 600 percent, and the growth of wheat exports from Baltimore had been even more dramatic.

From the outset Joseph Ellicott concentrated his attention on the improvement of the upstream site on Frederick Road, which became known as the Upper Mills. John, Andrew, and Andrew's sons undertook development of the lower stretch of river. Their household goods, tools, and farm implements were brought by boat from Philadelphia to Elkridge Landing. At that time, Elkridge Landing was the head of navigation on the Patapsco River and was a tobacco port from which ships sailed directly to England. From Elkridge, the Ellicotts' possessions were carried by wagon and then by wheelbarrow on a footpath

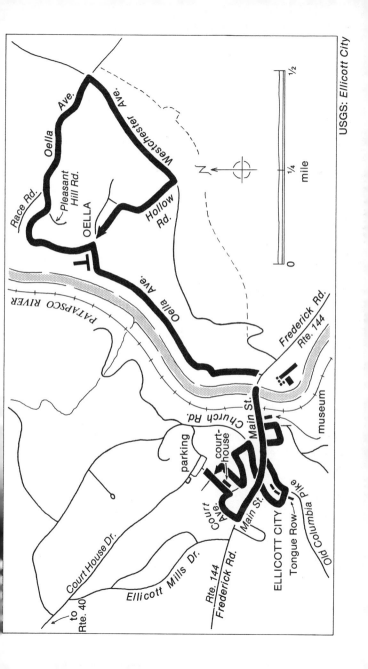

USGS: Ellicott City

PATAPSCO RIVER

Race Rd.

Oella Ave.

Pleasant Hill Rd.

OELLA

Hollow Rd.

Westchester Ave.

Oella Ave.

Frederick Rd.
Rte. 144

museum

Church Rd.

Main St.

parking

court-house

Court Ave.

Court House Dr.

to Rte. 40

Ellicott Mills Dr.

Rte. 144
Frederick Rd.

Main St.

ELLICOTT CITY

Tongue Row

Old Columbia Pike

mile

0   ¼   ½

along the river to the new settlement. Even the wagons themselves had to be disassembled and carried in.

By 1774 the Ellicotts had supervised the clearing of land and the construction of a low dam, a saw mill, a grist mill, and a log barracks for their workmen, whom they had hired to come with them from Pennsylvania. At first they grew and milled their own wheat in order to demonstrate to the surrounding planters that wheat could be cultivated and sold. Charles Carroll of Carrollton, a financial backer of the Ellicotts and the largest planter in Maryland, was among the first to convert from tobacco to wheat.

By the end of the American Revolution, the flow of wheat from nearby plantations to Ellicotts Lower Mills had increased to the point where the Ellicotts decided to export flour to England as soon as trade with the British could be resumed. In 1783 the Ellicotts built a wharf at the corner of Light and Pratt streets in Baltimore, where they used a dredge of their own invention to deepen the channel. They not only exported flour but also imported English ironware, tea, mirrors, dinner sets, glassware, linen, silks, satins, brocades, groceries, liquors, and wines, which they sold to the planters through their new store of Ellicott & Company at the Lower Mills. Planters throughout the region congregated at the store and post office, bringing their wheat in exchange for purchases.

In 1791 Ferdinand M. Bayard, a member of the French Academy of Arts and Sciences, recorded his impression of a visit to the Lower Mills:

> The river, upon the borders of which Mr. Ellicott has built his mill, is enclosed by two chains of uncultivated hills . . . The bottom of the river, whose channel can hardly be decried, is full of broken rocks which the waters have not yet worked smooth. Some masses are raised above the surface of the river, whose waters, dashing against them, keep up continually a dull noise, truly sepulchral. The advantages to be derived from a mill in this place render the proprietor insensible to the horrors which surround him. It can only be a regard for pecuniary interest which enables him to live undisturbed by the noise of the waters which dash over the rocks.

The leaness of the sheep and cattle attest to the poverty of the soil.
A miserable garden, from which the productions seem forced;
fields where the scantiness of the grain leaves the soil exposed;
plains incapable of producing a middling sized oak; such is the
melancholy aspect presented by the country from Baltimore to Ellicott's Mills.

In time, the Ellicotts erected iron-smelting furnaces, forges,
rolling mills, and nail factories in their stretch of the Patapsco
Valley. Other mills were added later for the production of copper sheathing. A Quaker meeting house and school were built.
After reading an article in a horticultural journal and conduct-
ing their own experiments with plaster, the Ellicotts instructed
the surrounding planters in the use of lime as a fertilizer to restore the exhausted soil. They imported blocks of gypsum from
Nova Scotia and ground it for fertilizer . They constructed
bridges and a road east to Baltimore at their own expense and,
with the assistance of Charles Carroll, they built a road west to
Carroll's vast Doughoregan Manor. Other planters helped to
extend the road to Frederick, opening the new wheat country
of the interior to Ellicotts Lower Mills. In 1804 the Baltimore
and Frederick Turnpike was established through the Lower
Mills, supplanting the old Frederick Road through the Upper
Mills. The turnpike was soon linked with the Ohio Valley by
the National Road through Cumberland and Wheeling, so that
by 1818, when the settlement numbered about three thousand
people, the country's most important land thoroughfare passed
through Ellicotts Lower Mills.

During the same period, granite quarrying became a significant industry. Between 1806 and 1821 granite for Baltimore
Cathedral—at the time one of the nation's most significant
structures because of its large size and distinguished neoclassic
design—was hauled from Ellicotts Lower Mills along the
Frederick Turnpike in huge wagons drawn by nine yoke of
oxen.

Ellicotts Lower Mills received another boost in 1827, when
the Baltimore & Ohio Railroad was incorporated by several

leading Baltimore merchants and bankers. They feared that the Erie Canal, completed in 1825, and the newly planned Chesapeake & Ohio Canal, with its terminus in Georgetown, would each divert commerce with the Great Lakes region and the Ohio Valley away from Baltimore. The first leg of the experimental railroad was laid up the Patapsco Valley, and Ellicotts Lower Mills was selected as its inland terminus until the line was extended farther westward.

During the next forty years Ellicotts Lower Mills continued to grow and prosper, although in the aftermath of the financial panic of 1837, one branch of the Ellicott family, "trading under the name of Jonathan Ellicott & Sons, being embarrassed in their circumstances and largely indebted to many individuals" (as recited in the deed of trust), was forced to convey the flour mill to trustees for the benefit of their creditors. Colonel Charles Carroll III acquired the mill in partnership with Charles A. Gambrill, who eventually became the firm's principal. The mill continued to be owned by the C. A. Gambrill Manufacturing Company until 1923, and during that period it was rebuilt at least twice after being destroyed by flood or damaged by fire. Most of the currently existing mill structure, still in use today, dates from 1917.

In 1840 Ellicotts Lower Mills was selected as the site of the courthouse for the new Howard District of what was then Anne Arundel County. In 1851 it was made the county seat when Howard County was organized. The Lower Mills became Ellicott City with the granting of a municipal charter in 1867. The next year, however, much of the city's industry was destroyed in a devastating flash flood, as described in Chapter 1. Although some of the mills were rebuilt, many were not, and the community never fully recovered economically.

AUTOMOBILE: Ellicott City is located west of Baltimore where Route 144 (Frederick Road) crosses the Patapsco River.

From Interstate 695 (the Beltway) west of Baltimore, take exit 15B for Route 40 west toward Ellicott City. Follow

Route 40 about 4.4 miles to an intersection with Route 99 (Rogers Avenue) at a traffic light. Turn left and go 1.1 miles, passing intersections where Rogers Avenue and then Ellicott Mills Drive turn right. Continue straight on Court House Drive to the large parking lots serving the Howard County courthouse.

WALK: From the courthouse parking lots, head toward the granite courthouse complex. Pass to the right of the court-house buildings (the front—or downhill—section was built in 1840–43), then turn downhill to the right on Court Avenue. At the bottom of Court Avenue, turn left onto Main Street and follow it down past the intersection with Old Columbia Pike. Continue downhill on Main Street to the depot square next to the railroad station museum; the discussion below mentions some of the buildings you will pass on the way.

The large granite building with the ironwork porch at 8202 Main Street is the Howard House, built as a hotel about 1850. Because it was carved into the hillside with its back door at ground level on the third floor, the hotel's central stairs became a thoroughfare between Main Street and Church Road on the way to and from the courthouse. The first floor, as later expanded, had a bar, a lunchroom, and an ice cream parlor. The second floor included a dining room for hotel guests and a separate banqueting hall. Following the construction of the railroad, tourists flocked to the town in order to combine the novelty of a train ride with a country excursion. Also, the granting of a municipal charter gave Ellicott City the right to license the sale of liquor. The city became the only "wet spot" in Howard County and the site of lavish parties.

Four doors down from the Howard House is the Walker-Chandler house, built about 1790. It has served successively as a private residence, a bootmaker's shop, offices, funeral home, tavern and dive, then offices again, before becoming Ellicotts Country Store.

At 8044 Main Street is the former Colonial Inn and Opera House, purportedly where John Wilkes Booth made his debut. Another prominent inn was the Patapsco Hotel at 8004–8026 Main Street, immediately adjacent to the railroad tracks. Rather than depositing the hotel's guests at the depot across the street, the train pulled forward a few dozen yards and made another stop at a platform along the side of the hotel's second floor, so that guests could enter the hotel directly from the railroad carriages.

From the depot square, continue east on Main Street under the railroad to the bridge over the Patapsco River.

The site of the original Ellicotts Lower Mills is now occupied by the Wilkins-Rogers flour mill and silos at the bend in the river downstream from the Frederick Road bridge. Most of the early settlement was on the east bank of the river but was destroyed by the flood of 1868. The row of houses where thirty-six people died (as discussed in Chapter 1) stood between the mill and higher ground. Opposite the mill near Frederick Road are the remains of the stone house of George Ellicott, a son of Andrew Ellicott.

Back on the west bank of the Patapsco, between the river and the railroad, is another old stone structure, believed to have been originally built as a house for mill hands. For a period during the nineteenth century it served as Radcliffe's Emporium, a general store. Neighboring houses upstream were swept away by the flood of 1868.

The mill village of Oella, mentioned at the outset of this chapter, is located on Oella Avenue about 0.7 mile upstream from the eastern end of the bridge over the Patapsco River. Oella is well worth touring by car at the end of your walk in Ellicott City, and directions are provided at the end of this chapter.

For now, however, return to the depot square and railroad station in Ellicott City.

The B&O station dates from 1831, when the railroad first reached Ellicotts Lower Mills. The building has been restored to its early nineteenth-century appearance and now houses the B&O Railroad Station Museum.

From the curved stone wall next to the railroad station museum, cross the street and enter the alley opposite. Turn right over Tiber Run then left onto Main Street. At the next intersection, turn left up Old Columbia Pike and continue to Tongue Row, a group of stone houses (now shops) built by a Mr. Tongue in the early 1800s.

From Tongue Row, descend on narrow stairs between the buildings. Bear right by a parking lot and return to Main Street. Cross Main Street and climb half-right up Church Road past the former firehouse (now the public library) where leather buckets and other hand equipment were once kept. Turn left opposite the Emory United Methodist Church. Turn left again to climb past the small offices of Lawyers Row and the former First Presbyterian Church, now the headquarters of the Howard County Historical Society. Turn right past the courthouse and return to the parking lot.

As noted earlier, the village of Oella, which in physical terms remains an enclave of mill housing surrounding the former textile plant, is located on the east bank of the Patapsco River about 0.75 mile upstream from Frederick Road. Oella got its start in 1808 when the founders of the Union Manufacturing Company of Maryland (the first corporation to be chartered by the state legislature) purchased land and started selling stock. By October 1809, the first textile mill had been completed. In 1811 the company had its property resurveyed under the name of "Oella," which the patent said was "in commemoration of the first woman who applied herself to the spinning of cotton on the continent of America." However, the identity of this mysterious (or fabled) Oella has yet to be discovered.

The Union dam (now breached at its western end) is located about 1.3 miles upstream from the village and just below the Route 40 bridge. From the dam a millrace, constructed with slave labor and said to be one of the longest races feeding a single mill in the country, runs along the eastern bank of the river to Oella, creating a vertical drop at the mill of nearly 50 feet. The mill generated its own power until the construction of Liberty Dam in the early 1950s diminished the flow of water.

For a time, the Union mill at Oella was among the nation's largest makers of cotton goods, but in 1889 financial difficulties forced its sale to William J. Dickey of the Dickeyville mills, who converted the plant to making woolen fabric. In 1918 the three main mill buildings and a warehouse burned down, but these structures were replaced by a new mill that was later expanded several times and still stands. The plant prospered during World War II, employing (as of January 1945) 382 people working in three shifts. Production for 1945 was 445,471 yards of woolen cloth of which 60 percent was for military coats. Operations at Oella reached their peak in the 1950s, when the plant employed 500 workers producing fancy woolen fabrics for men's sport coats and suits. In the 1960s, however, the upsurge in imported textiles and synthetics engulfed domestic woolen manufacturers. The decline at Oella became even more precipitous with the advent of double-knit fabrics that could not be produced on the machinery used there. The plant was closed in 1972.

For the decade following the mill's closing, the future of Oella even as a residential community was in doubt because there was no public water or sewer system. Raw sewage from the mill housing was pumped into leaky septic tanks, and for a period Baltimore County considered condemning much of the mill housing. Eventually, however, the county installed water and sewer lines through the rocky terrain at a cost of more than $5 million. Now the community, where low-paid mill employees had lived for generations, is in the throes of gentrification as the old housing is restored and other enterprises, many of an arts-and-crafts nature, occupy the mill.

AUTOMOBILE: To reach Oella from the Howard County Courthouse parking lots, follow Court House Drive back toward Route 40. After 0.5 mile turn left off Court House Drive onto Ellicott Mills Drive. Descend steeply 0.5 mile, then turn left onto Frederick Road (Main Street) at a T-intersection. Go 0.4 mile downhill through Ellicott City and across the bridge over the Patapsco River. After crossing the bridge, turn immediately left onto Oella Avenue.

Follow Oella Avenue past the low shelf of land that was the site of the Ellicott Iron Works at the beginning of the nineteenth century and later the site of the Granite Cotton Mill, which was destroyed by the flood of 1868 (see Chapter 1). Continue on Oella Avenue along the side of the valley above the river and past mill housing. Bear right past the large mill, then turn sharply left so as to continue around the mill. Follow the road past more mill housing. Curve right and continue past intersections with Pleasant Hill Road on the right and Race Road on the left. Eventually, turn right near the rim of the valley onto Westchester Avenue. Go 0.4 mile, then turn right downhill onto Hollow Road; Hollow Road is steep, curved, and two-way, so go very slowly. At the bottom of the hill, fork left past the mill to return to Frederick Road the way you came.

4

PATAPSCO VALLEY STATE PARK

Daniels

Walking and ski touring—3.0 to 6.5 miles (4.8 to 10.5 kilometers) depending on how far you continue past Daniels. Follow the remains of Alberton Road (now closed to cars) west along the winding Patapsco Valley to the dam and ruined mill complex at Daniels. Although the mill buildings at Daniels are privately owned and closed to the public, they are easily viewed from the park path. A spur trail leads a short distance to the stone remains of St. Stanislaus Kostka Chapel. From Daniels, the broad trail continues upstream and eventually turns into a narrow and somewhat rugged footpath through a particularly isolated section of the valley. Return the way you came. The park is open daily from sunrise to sunset. Dogs must be leashed. Managed by the Maryland Park Service (telephone 461–5005).

FIVE HUNDRED FIFTY ACRES fronting on the Patapsco River. A factory complex consisting of a three-story stone mill, 48 by 230 feet, and various larger but lower brick and cement-block structures for the manufacture of heavy canvas, denim, industrial belting, and hose. A concrete dam furnishing 400 horsepower and generating surplus electricity sold to the Baltimore Gas and Electric Company. A post office, a community hall, and a general store. And 118 single-family, two-family, and rowhouse dwellings, most of them brick, averaging five rooms each, many without interior plumbing. In 1940, this was

Alberton. Before that, the town was called Elysville. It has since been renamed Daniels. For three generations it had been the company town of James S. Gary & Sons. But on November 23, 1940, the entire town was sold—houses, factory, and machinery—to the C. R. Daniels Company of Newark, New Jersey, for $65,000 at an auction held in front of the general store to foreclose Gary & Sons' default under its mortgage. The company simply had been unable to survive the Depression.

A few years later, however, stimulated by the immense demand for canvas and denim during World War II, the factory was again humming. Operations continued until the floodwaters of Tropical Storm Agnes churned through the mill in 1972, but not before the Daniels Company itself, in a remarkable exercise of milltown proprietorship, had razed all the houses in 1968, destroying a town since named to the Register of Historic Places, evicting about a quarter of the mill's employees and many of its pensioners, but perhaps saving their lives and certainly their property from the subsequent devastation of Agnes.

Elysville got its start in the 1840s when the Elysville Manufacturing Company, consisting of Thomas Ely and his four brothers, started building the original stone mill, now roofless and gutted but with walls still standing. The Baltimore & Ohio Railroad already passed through the stretch of curving valley bottom. Constructing, equipping, and operating the mill were more costly than anticipated, and in 1845 the Ely brothers decided to convey it to a new corporation funded with more capital from additional shareholders. Accordingly, in 1846 the Elysville Company sold the mill to the newly-incorporated Okisko Company in exchange for $25,000 of Okisko stock. Five Baltimore merchants, who would soon wish they had never heard of Thomas Ely and his slippery brothers, paid another $25,000 for their shares in Okisko.

Further improvements were made, the fresh capital was spent, but still the enterprise floundered. In 1849 a suit was brought by unpaid contractors and other creditors demanding

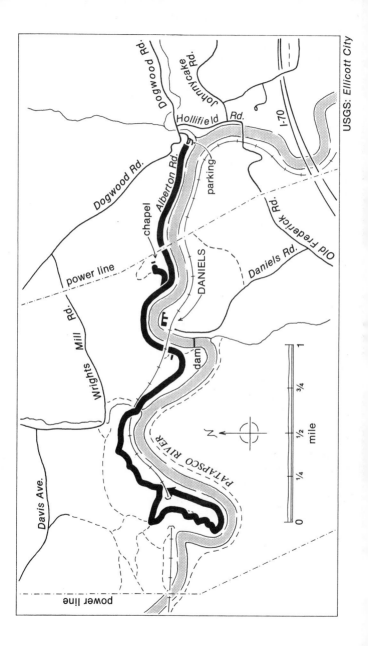

USGS: *Ellicott City*

that the mill be sold to satisfy their claims. At this point the Elysville Company brought its own suit asserting that the sale of the mill to Okisko was a nullity and urging that the mill, complete with $25,000 in additional improvements, be returned to the Elys or sold for their benefit on the grounds that the contract with Okisko had required that the Elysville Company be paid in cash and not stock, that Thomas Ely (as president of the Ely Corporation) had lacked power to sell the mill, and that the Elysville Corporation had been without charter authority to hold stock in another company such as Okisko. When the court attempted to sell the property, Hugh Ely, a state senator who was one of the brothers, bought the mill at the auction but then repudiated his purchase on the ground that the advertisement describing the property, which was based on an inventory that the Ely brothers themselves had prepared when selling the mill to Okisko, was inaccurate and misleading. Hugh Ely also testified in the principal case, but in its opinion the Court pointedly concluded that his testimony was utterly beyond credence. The intertwined litigation dragged on until 1853, reaching the state's highest court three times. The property was finally sold for the benefit of creditors.

During the 1850s, the mill was bought and sold by a succession of corporations, some of them simply reorganizations of prior owners. For a time, the property was owned by the Alberton Manufacturing Company, one of whose principals was Jacob Albert, an Okisko creditor whose name stuck to the community. Late in the decade, the mill and the town came under the firm control of James S. Gary, a self-made man whose fortune propelled his son, James A. Gary, to the position of Postmaster General for President McKinley and to leadership of the Maryland Republican party until his death in 1920.

Under Gary ownership, the mill at Alberton became a solid financial success for the first time, helped by large contracts for tents during the Civil War. In 1860 the mill employed fifty men and 120 women and owned 120 looms and 3000 spindles. An oakum factory was also in operation making caulking from cotton waste. By 1895 the mill had grown to 340 looms, presumably run by an equal number of women and children. (During the 1890s, the Maryland cotton manufacturing industry employed more children under age sixteen than any other type of manufacturer, with an average starting age of twelve.) By 1915 more than 400 hands were employed at Alberton.

During most of the period between the Civil War and World War I, the mill and the surrounding town were managed by Samuel F. Cobb, remembered by his former workers and subordinates as an Old Testament-like figure with a long white beard who was not only boss but *de facto* mayor as well, summoning outside authority only as need arose. Cobb's diaries describe the practice of sending recruiters to Virginia and West Virginia to attract employees—especially families with many girls, since inexpensive female labor was preferred. One recruiter purportedly enticed a family to move to Alberton to work in the mill by telling them that bananas, free for the picking, grew in the surrounding woods. When the new employees complained to Mr. Cobb that there were no bananas, he is said to have replied that the monkeys had eaten them all. Although almost certainly apocryphal, the story nonetheless may accurately reflect the tenor of Mr. Cobb's regime.

The company policy for management of the mill was a combination of long hours and low wages matched by equally low rents for large and comfortable houses. Even as late as 1968, the C. R. Daniels Company was charging a top rent of $4.50 per week for a seven-room house, provided that the head of the family worked in the mill. The company also provided free firewood, Christmas gifts for children, a school, and support for a growing variety of community activities.

Aside from the mill, the center of town life was the churches. James A. Gary built the Gary United Methodist Church on the hill south of the mill in 1879 as a memorial to his father. It is the only building in the community undamaged by flood or fire, and its congregation still includes some former mill employees. Other churches were encouraged, including the Catholic chapel of St. Stanislaus Kostka, whose priest sometimes skated down the frozen river from the Woodstock Seminary to conduct Sunday service. In the 1920s the chapel was struck by lightning and burned. Its ruins are located on the hillside across the river and slightly downstream from the mill. An Episcopal congregation existed until World War I. Its stone church was later incorporated into the mill complex and is most easily seen from the side of the factory that is farthest downstream. In 1940 a small Pentecostal church was built near the railroad bridge across the river from the mill. At one point during the 1972 flood, only the roof and tower of the church were visible. Dozens of company houses used to front the road above and below the church, which still stands today. The residents crossed to the mill on a pedestrian suspension bridge like the one at Orange Grove, discussed in Chapter 2.

Following World War I, the company's business began to decline as the owners failed to modernize the mill. During the Depression, operations nearly stopped altogether. Many employees worked only one or two days a week. Gary & Sons obtained a loan from the federal government's Reconstruction Finance Corporation, but when the firm was unable to keep up with the payments, the entire enterprise was sold to the C. R. Daniels Company. Daniels renovated the mill and much of the housing but eventually announced that it was going to demolish the dwellings because it could not afford the cost of still further repairs and improvements—estimated at $750,000—in order to bring the residences up to housing code standards. Despite an outcry from local anti-poverty agencies and historic preservation groups, the town ceased to exist in 1968 although the mill continued in business.

In 1972 Agnes struck. The water rose so fast that five people were caught in the mill building and had to be evacuated from the roof by helicopter. The town store was pushed off its foundation and swept away. When the flood receded, cars, trucks, flotsam, and wreckage were left heaped against the buildings, which were coated inside and out with mud. Snarls of nylon yarn trailed from windows and the tops of telephone poles. The

C. R. Daniels Company suffered an uninsured loss of $2.7 million and pulled out of the valley. Then in 1977, the mill, while being used as a warehouse, was gutted by fire. Since then a few structures have been repaired in part and used by a variety of businesses. Across the river, where much of Elysville-Alberton-Daniels used to stand, the land has been incorporated into the Patapsco Valley State Park.

AUTOMOBILE: The section of the Patapsco Valley State Park explored by this walk is located west of Baltimore upstream from where Interstate 70 and Old Frederick Road cross the river. The trailhead is on Alberton Road, which intersects with Dogwood Road at the point where Dogwood Road most closely approaches the Patapsco River.

From Interstate 695 (the Beltway) west of Baltimore, take exit 17 for Security Boulevard, then fork toward Rolling Road. Follow Security Boulevard west past Security Square Mall and the intersection with Rolling Road. Continue straight west on Security Boulevard 0.3 mile beyond the intersection with Rolling Road, then turn left onto Greengage Road. Follow Greengage Road 0.3 mile, then turn right onto Fairbrook Road. Follow Fairbrook Road 0.4 mile, then turn left onto Johnnycake Road. Follow Johhnycake Road 1.4 miles as the road eventually winds downhill into the Patapsco Valley. At a T-intersection with Hollifield Road in front of the river, turn right. Go 0.3 mile to a T-intersection with Dogwood Road. Turn left over a bridge, then turn left immediately onto Alberton Road toward Daniels. With caution, follow Alberton Road about 150 yards to an oval drive in front of a house. Turn left to park as far from the house as possible. As a courtesy to the owners of this house, do not park in their oval drive, nor anywhere near the green park gate. Finally, if "no parking" signs are posted, park elsewhere—such as the shoulder of Alberton Road near the intersection with Dogwood Road.

The starting point at Alberton Road can also be reached from Interstate 70 by taking exit 87B for Route 29 north to-

ward Route 99. Route 29 also provides a good approach
from the vicinity of Columbia. Follow Route 29 north to its
end at a T-intersection with Route 99, and there turn right
(east). Go 0.6 mile on Route 99, then turn left onto Old
Frederick Road. Follow Old Frederick Road 1.7 miles as
the road eventually descends into the Patapsco Valley and
crosses the river. About 100 yards beyond the bridge, continue straight on Hollifield Road where Johnnycake Road
intersects from the right. Continue 0.3 mile to a T-
intersection with Dogwood Road. Turn left over a bridge,
then turn left immediately onto Alberton Road toward Daniels. With caution, follow Alberton Road about 150 yards
to an oval drive in front of a house. Turn left to park as far
from the house as possible. As a courtesy to the owners of
this house, do not park in their oval drive, nor anywhere
near the green park gate. Finally, if "no parking" signs
are posted, park elsewhere—such as the shoulder of Alberton Road near the intersection with Dogwood Road.

WALK: With the Patapsco River toward your left, follow
the remains of Alberton Road past a gate. Continue along
the road upstream for about 1.0 mile to Daniels.
    Where you first come opposite the ruins of Daniels, a
road intersects from the rear-right. This road leads uphill
and around the shoulder of a ravine to the left. The ruins of
the old Catholic chapel of St. Stanislaus Kostka are located in the woods on the far side of the ravine shortly
after the road bends left away from the river.
    From the riverside road opposite Daniels, continue
around the big bend in the river. After passing under the
railroad, do not follow the main trail where it curves
abruptly right uphill next to the railroad; instead, continue
straight on a less worn trail. Follow this trail (quite narrow
at some points) as it gradually curves right past several
side trails that lead left toward the Daniels dam. The path
eventually rejoins the river on the left, then joins the rail-

*road. Be alert for trains, and do not walk on the tracks; if
a train passes, stand well back.*

*With the river on your left and the railroad tracks on
your right, follow an old railbed a short distance to a
bridge over a stream. Immediately after crossing the
bridge, cross the railroad tracks, then follow a path that
climbs along the side of the valley. With the river toward
your left, continue along the side of the valley for about 0.7
mile. Rejoin the railroad just before a tunnel, but veer
right immediately to follow the path uphill away from the
railroad. When the path levels off, turn left at a four-way
trail junction. Follow the path up across the top of the hill
through which the railroad tunnel passes. Continue as the
path narrows and zigzags downhill. (At one point the trail
splits, but soon rejoins.) Continue steeply downhill to the
bottom of the valley.*

*With the river on your right, follow the path downstream
through the bottom of the curving valley until the trail
gradually rises to join the railroad near the mouth of the
tunnel. With caution, cross the tracks and rejoin the trail
that you followed earlier in the opposite direction. With the
river toward your right, follow the trail back along the valley to Daniels and your starting point at Alberton Road.*

Ellicotts Upper Mills

While you are in the vicinity of the Daniels walk, you may be
interested to know that the point where the Old Frederick Road
crosses the Patapsco River was formerly Ellicotts Upper Mills.
As noted briefly in Chapter 3, the Upper Mills were purchased
by the Ellicott family in 1774 from James Hood, who in 1768
had built a dam and mill for grinding corn. Four years earlier
the Ellicotts had bought undeveloped land farther downstream
at what became the Lower Mills and later Ellicott City. At that
time the Upper Mills was more valuable than the Lower Mills
because it was located where the main road linking Baltimore

and Frederick forded the river. When the Ellicott property was divided, the Upper Mills was assigned to Joseph Ellicott, the oldest of the three Ellicott brothers. Ironically, nothing now remains at the Upper Mills.

When Joseph Ellicott moved his family from Pennsylvania to Maryland in 1775, he tore down the mill built by James Hood and constructed another for milling wheat using the latest inventions and improvements, many of his own design. On the shelf of land at the west end of the present bridge, he also built a large house and (on land later taken by the railroad) an ornamental garden with a fish pond and fountain spouting water ten feet high. When the Upper Mills tract was resurveyed in 1797, it was called "Fountainville."

Like his brothers at the Lower Mills, Joseph also built a general store that sold dry goods, silks, satins, and brocades, as well as the usual groceries. Although the store reportedly did a good business, society must have been limited. Four of Joseph's nine children married the orphaned brothers and sisters of the Evans family, whom the Ellicotts had brought with them from Pennsylvania.

When Joseph Ellicott settled at the Upper Mills, he was already wealthy, having traveled to England ten years before to claim and liquidate his great-grandfather's estate to which he was heir. In Pennsylvania he had been high sheriff of Bucks County and a member of the provincial assembly. His preoccupation with mathematics, clockmaking, mill works, and mechanics had also earned him prominence in scientific circles, and it is said that as he got older, these interests almost completely precluded social intercourse even with his own family. One of his projects was a four-faced musical grandfather clock that played twenty-four tunes and marked seconds, minutes, hours, days, months and years, phases of the moon, and motions of the planets.

Joseph died in 1780 but his widow, Judith, maintained her household at the Upper Mills until her death in 1809. By then the mill and store had greatly declined in value. The Frederick

Turnpike had been relocated through the Lower Mills. This, in time, utterly eclipsed the small settlement farther upstream.

5

PATAPSCO VALLEY STATE PARK

McKeldin Recreation Area

Walking—4.0 miles (6.4 kilometers). Follow well-marked footpaths through the deep valleys and woods at the confluence of the South and North branches of the Patapsco River. A spur trail leads to McKeldin Falls, among the largest of our local cascades. The McKeldin Area provides one of the best opportunities for walking in the Baltimore region. The park opens daily at 10 AM during the colder months and at 8 AM during the warmer months. The park closes at sunset year-round, and is also closed on Christmas. An admission fee is charged on weekends during March through October. Dogs are prohibited. Managed by the Maryland Park Service (telephone 461–5005).

"**F**RANKLY, I LIKE THE SOUND of the Governor Theodore R. McKeldin Recreation Area," said Governor Theodore R. McKeldin at the dedication ceremony for this section of the Patapsco Valley State Park in 1957. For more than a decade McKeldin had been one of the leading advocates for the expansion of the park to include the entire Patapsco Valley downstream from Sykesville as well as the North Branch below Liberty Reservoir. As governor, McKeldin was in the enviable position of being able to implement what he described as a "brilliant plan" for park expansion that he had come across after taking office—a plan developed earlier at his recommen-

dation while mayor of Baltimore but shelved by the previous governor. The plan called for the extension into the greater Baltimore area of the system of stream valley parks first proposed in the Olmstead Brothers report fifty years earlier (discussed in Chapter 19).

Prior to the 1950s, the Patapsco Valley State Park included less than 1500 acres in a patchwork between Route 40 (Hollofield) and Route 1 (Avalon). The park—or Patapsco River Forest Reserve as it was at first called—had started with a gift to the state of 434 acres in 1907, at a time when President Theodore Roosevelt (for whom McKeldin was named) and his chief forester, Gifford Pinchot, were popularizing the philosophy of conservation and were adding millions of acres of land to federal ownership, withdrawing immense public tracts from sale, and setting apart federal forest reserves. In 1912 the state legislature appropriated funds for the first time for the purchase of forest lands to be managed by the Maryland State Board of Forestry. By the time of the Depression during the 1930s, the Patapsco River Forest Reserve included about 1300 acres; during this period the area was improved with trails, picnic grounds, shelters, and campsites constructed by workers of the federally sponsored Civilian Conservation Corps. As the primary use of the area shifted from forest preservation to recreation, the name was changed to the Patapsco Valley State Park under the newly consolidated Department of State Forests and Parks.

In 1946 the Patapsco River Valley Commission, appointed by then-Mayor McKeldin, drew up a plan for enlarging the state park to 15,000 acres connected by a riverside parkway. The road was never built but other aspects of the plan reappeared in a study prepared by private consultants for the Maryland State Planning Commission in 1950. The new plan called for a linear park of 8500 acres averaging half a mile in width and extending 37 miles along the river from the Hanover Street Bridge in Baltimore to Sykesville. Improvements were to include not only the usual hiking and riding trails and pic-

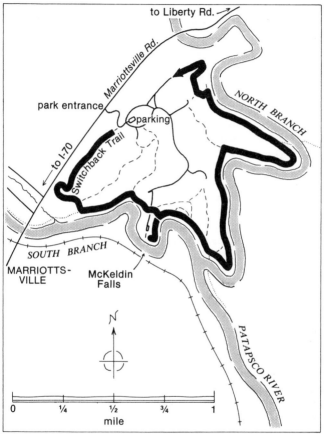

to Liberty Rd.

Marriottsville Rd.

park entrance

parking

to I-70

Switchback Trail

NORTH BRANCH

SOUTH BRANCH

MARRIOTTS-
VILLE

McKeldin
Falls

PATAPSCO RIVER

N

0   ¼   ½   ¾   1
mile

USGS: *Sykesville, Ellicott City*

nicking and camping facilities but also golf courses (even min-iature golf), swimming pools, a miniature railroad, a carousel, dance pavilions, restaurants, cabins, and lodges. The total cost was estimated at $6 million and a period of twelve years was thought sufficient to complete the project.

During the next twenty-five years the park grew in fits and starts. For a period, land acquisition stalled at about 4500 acres as funds were exhausted and state and local officials and a citi-zen advisory committee debated which land should be given priority for purchase. A major area of contention was the marsh along the lower Patapsco, where gravel mining had left a series of small lakes in the flats beside the river. (This area has since been acquired at the urging of officials of Anne Arun-del County and, although not yet developed for recreation, it promises to be one of the most unusual and interesting sections of the park). By 1972, when much of the Patapsco Valley was devastated by Tropical Storm Agnes, the park included about 7000 acres spread between Baltimore, Howard, Carroll, and Anne Arundel counties and was visited yearly by an estimated 4.5 million people.

Yet at the same time that millions of dollars were being spent to expand the park, industrial pollution and suburban growth were turning the Patapsco River into a regional sewer. At first the problem was not without drollery. Children who swam at Ellicott City in the early 1900s had to post a lookout on the rocks upstream to warn the others to get out of the water when the Dickey Mill at Oella released dye into the river. But by mid-century swimming was unthinkable. Sykesville, Ellicott City, and other communities and institutional facilities dumped their untreated waste into the river. Newspaper accounts during the 1960s reported floating islands of bubbling sludge and a river bottom coated with decomposing matter. Massive fish kills occurred annually during periods of particularly toxic dis-charges. By 1967 a study by the Maryland Department of Water Resources classified the Patapsco River below Ilchester as "grossly polluted."

Since then, however, water quality in the Patapsco has improved significantly. Industries and most communities along the river have been required to connect into the large Patapsco interceptor sewer line that during the late 1960s was run up the valley from the Patapsco Wastewater Treatment Plant at Wagners Point. Also, the torrent caused by Tropical Storm Agnes flushed the accumulated filth from the riverbed (and dumped it in Chesapeake Bay). Still, however, incidents of industrial pollution and sewage overflows occur regularly, and sediments from erosion and stormwater runoff give the water its characteristic murky appearance.

After the 1972 Agnes flood, the Maryland Department of Natural Resources (into which the old Department of Forests and Parks had been incorporated) undertook to re-evaluate previous park plans for the Patapsco. The job was assigned to the Department's own staff in the Division of Land Planning Services. Working with members of the Maryland Park Service and a newly appointed citizen advisory committee, the state's design team developed a revised master plan on the basis of which the General Assembly in 1980 authorized a park totaling 15,200 acres, of which 12,626 had been acquired as of the beginning of 1987.

Aside from calling for a larger park, the current Patapsco master plan is generally more austere than earlier plans. The Department of Natural Resources has adopted the policy that the chief purpose of state parks is to promote the enjoyment and protection of natural, historic, and scenic features rather than to provide tennis courts, swimming pools, golf courses, and other recreation facilities that are more appropriately the responsibility of local governments (although the Patapsco plan has entailed acquisition of an existing golf course and several pools).

Finally, the park is being expanded beyond the immediate valley. The state had previously concentrated on buying only the valley bottom and slopes because they were visually and environmentally sensitive—and in most cases cheap as well.

The current plan calls for development of extensive campgrounds and picnic areas set back from the valley rim in areas that are beyond the reach of floods, easily accessible from nearby roads, and yet visually isolated in the woods. The valley slopes and bottomland will be reserved for low-cost improvements and low-key uses, such as riding and walking trails. The Park Service also hopes to build a nature interpretation center in the McKeldin Recreation Area.

AUTOMOBILE: The McKeldin Recreation Area of the Patapsco Valley State Park is located west of Baltimore below Liberty Reservoir. The entrance is on Marriottsville Road north of Marriottsville.

From Interstate 695 (the Beltway) west of Baltimore, take exit 16 for Interstate 70 west toward Frederick. Follow Interstate 70 west about 8.0 miles to exit 83 for Marriottsville Road. Bear right and follow Marriottsville Road north 4.0 miles to the park entrance on the right. Park your car in the lot just beyond the small ranger station at the top of the entrance road.

The park entrance can also be reached from the intersection of Liberty Road and Marriottsville Road west of Randallstown. In this case, follow Marriottsville Road southwest 4.7 miles.

WALK: From the parking lot and ranger station at the top of the entrance road, follow the entrance road back downhill toward Marriottsville Road for 70 yards. At the first bend, veer left off the road onto a wide path entering the woods. This is the Switchback Trail and it is marked with yellow and white blazes. Except for a few stretches noted below, the route described here follows this trail.

Follow the path through the woods, then down and around to the left by Marriottsville Road. Continue along the bottom of the slope. At the next trail junction, the yellow and white blazes indicate a path leading uphill to the left, but unless the river is in flood or you wish to maximize the length of your walk, continue straight downhill to the river's edge. You will rejoin the blazed trail later.

Turn left along the valley bottom. Eventually, turn right at a T-intersection and rejoin the blazed trail. Follow the path along the river bank, then up and straight across an asphalt road. Descend through the woods, at one point forking right downhill where the blazed trail veers left. At the river's edge, a spur trail along the bank leads upstream several hundred yards to McKeldin Falls.

With the river on your right, follow the riverside path downstream and across a large bare rock sloping into the river; if, however, you prefer not to cross the rocky slope, retrace your steps 50 yards and detour up and around the rock and back down to the path by the river. As you continue downstream, be alert for areas where the path is in danger of caving into the river because of erosion.

Follow the riverside path downstream to the confluence of the South and North branches of the Patapsco River. With the river on your right, follow the North Branch upstream. After about 0.7 mile, fork right and continue with the river on your right. Follow the path along the valley bottom, around to the left, and along the river. Eventually, the trail crosses a jumble of rocks shortly before the river bends slightly to the right. After about 220 yards, turn left to climb steeply away from the river. If you run into a cliff blocking further progress along the river's edge, you will know that you have gone too far and should retrace your steps 70 yards.

Follow the footpath as it climbs steeply away from the river and turns right. Continue obliquely uphill along the side of the valley. At an intersection near the crest of the slope, turn right. Follow the blazed path along the top of the slope, then gradually downhill and to the right along the side of the valley. Continue as the trail gradually climbs, then curves sharply left. Follow the path to a picnic

area and then along an asphalt road that at one point provides a view of Liberty Dam to the north. Continue straight to the parking lot by the ranger station. Be alert for cars.

6

SOLDIERS DELIGHT NATURAL ENVIRONMENT AREA

Walking and ski touring—3.0 to 5.0 miles (4.8 to 8.0 kilometers) depending on whether you continue west of Deer Park Road. A network of trails explores an unusual landscape of rocky meadows and stunted, piney woods. The park is open daily from sunrise to sunset. Dogs must be leashed. Managed by the Maryland Park Service (telephone 922–3044); if no answer, call Patapsco Valley State Park (461–5005).

THERE'S CHROME IN THEM THAR HILLS at Soldiers Delight.

Perhaps this news lacks the galvanic impact of a gold strike, but the fact remains that during the second quarter of the nineteenth century, ownership of chromite mines in the Soldiers Delight district northwest of Baltimore and at other outcroppings of serpentine rock in Maryland and southeastern Pennsylvania enabled Isaac Tyson, Jr., founder of the Baltimore Chrome Works, to control the world chromium market and become a very wealthy man.

The serpentine formations that break the surface in a few locations north and west of Baltimore are like nothing else in the region. They are commonly called serpentine *barrens,* and appropriately so. Blackjack oak, post oak, and Virginia pine (all small, drought-tolerant species) grow in the meager soil. Scattered through the woods are meadows of yellow grass. The faded colors and stunted forest offer hikers a refreshing change from the deep-soiled farmland, river gorges, and tall deciduous

woods so typical of Maryland's Piedmont region. Birdwatchers will be disappointed with the dearth of species, but botanists can roll and revel in the Indian grass, beard grass, turkeyfoot, and broom sedge. Depending on the season, visitors can also find bird's-foot violets, blazing stars, sundrops, Belgian asters, knotweed, goldenrod, fringed gentian, and many other flowers.

Serpentine is a greenish metamorphic rock found near Baltimore not only in the Soldiers Delight region but also in the Bare Hills west of Lake Roland. At Cardiff in Harford County, serpentine is quarried and sold under the trade name of Maryland Green Marble, although it is not a limestone, as are true marbles. The rock is used primarily for interior trim in banks, hotels, and office buildings (including the lobby of the Empire State Building). Serpentine has also been tried as a structural building stone, despite the tendency of the rock surface to flake off due to weathering. The exterior of the Mount Vernon Place Methodist Church, which has a distinctly greenish hue, is built of local serpentine.

More significantly, the occurrence of serpentine in Maryland is associated with the presence of chromium. In 1808 or 1810 chromium ore was discovered in the serpentine outcroppings at the Bare Hills estate of Jesse Tyson, a wealthy flour and grain merchant. The Tysons' gardener showed some black rocks to Tyson's son, Isaac, who was a student of geology, mineralogy, and chemistry. He identified the rocks as chromite, and analysis established that the ore was of a salable grade.

With financial assistance from his father, the young Tyson started mining the ore on a small scale. Ore was extracted at the Bare Hills as early as 1811, and by 1817 Tyson was also mining chromite from stream deposits (called placers) in the serpentine barrens at Soldiers Delight. As with gold mining, the stream sands were washed in a sluice (called a buddle) to concentrate the heavy chromite. The ore was then shipped to paint and ceramic factories in England, for at that time chro-

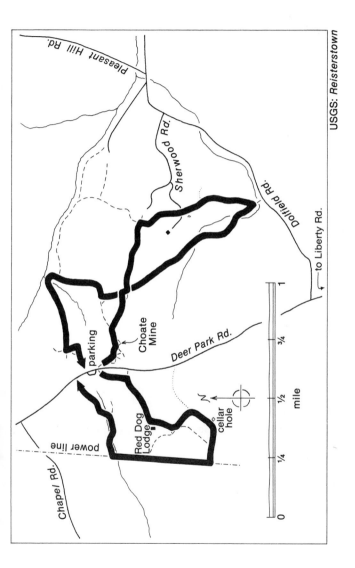

USGS: *Reisterstown*

mium was used primarily to make brilliant pigments, dyes, and glazes (hence chrome-yellow, chrome-orange, chrome-green, and other chrome hues).

Chromite mining was only a small part of Tyson's business as a manufacturer of chemicals and medicines, but in 1827 he hit pay dirt. He noticed that a cider barrel that had been brought in a wagon to Belair Market in Baltimore was steadied by rocks that he recognized as chromite. He traced the stone to the Reed farm near Jarrettsville in Harford County, obtained mineral rights to the property, and there, at what came to be called Chrome Hill, found a massive deposit of ore only eight feet below the surface. The Reed Mine was developed quickly and became so profitable that Tyson temporarily suspended his operations at other sites.

Tyson continued, however, to search out serpentine formations in Maryland and Pennsylvania, and he bought or leased property wherever there were indications of chromium. Not long after the Reed discovery, Tyson opened the Wood Mine in the State Line District of Lancaster County, Pennsylvania. This operation was another bonanza, eventually proving to be the richest chromium mine in the United States. Isaac Tyson's mines were far more productive and economical than other sources, with the result that between 1828 and 1850 virtually all of the chromium used in the world came from his mines.

Tyson's search for chromite also led to his involvement in the mining and smelting of iron and copper. In league with his partners, he eventually owned most of the copper deposits in Maryland. He visited pits, smelting plants, and iron works up and down the East Coast. He was a leader in the use of new and more efficient methods of refining ore, such as smelting with hard coal, and pre-heating air to create a hot blast. Engrossed with mining and minerals, he or his agents investigated deposits and mining claims from Maine to Virginia, west to Arkansas and Missouri, and even in Cuba and Spain. "I am now going to Stafford in Vermont and for what purpose?" he wrote in his journal on December 1, 1833:

All for the sake of gain and how great the sacrifice. My beloved wife not yet out of her bed and requiring the sympathy and solace of her husband. My little children requiring the care and attention of their father & my business neglected. . . . I am able to talk philosophically on these subjects and show the unreasonableness of avarice and the folly of accumulating wealth for children and yet I find myself pursuing the beaten track.

In 1845 Tyson and his associates established the Baltimore Chrome Works for the manufacture of chromium compounds from raw ore. The plant was located on Block Street at the entrance to the Inner Harbor, south of what is now Little Italy. Tyson's timing in this venture was fortunate because the export market for unprocessed ore began to decline after the discovery of high-grade chromite in Turkey in 1848 by a geologist who had gained some of his experience working for Tyson. Although the export of chrome ore from the United States had practically ceased by 1860, the manufacture of chromium compounds continued to prosper and was carried on by Tyson's sons after his death in 1861. Local mines were eventually closed as the Baltimore Chrome Works obtained ore more cheaply from company-owned mines in California and later in New Caledonia. Until a rival plant was established in Philadelphia in 1882, the Baltimore Chrome Works supplied virtually all the chromium chemicals used by American industry.

Tyson's principal operation at Soldiers Delight was the Choate Mine. It was opened before 1839 and was worked intermittently until about 1886. It consisted of an inclined shaft sloping to the southwest for as much as 200 feet and fanning out to a mine face 160 feet wide. During the chromium shortage caused by World War I, when the mineral was needed for high-grade steel, the Choate Mine was reopened for a brief period, but was again closed with the signing of the armistice. The mine entrance is still visible but the sloping shaft should not be entered.

As for the old Baltimore Chrome Works, in 1908 the company combined with two rival firms to form the Mutual Chem-

ical Company of America. During the next half-cen
tual greatly expanded its Inner Harbor plant for process
chromium compounds, and in the early 1950s the facility was
the world's largest chromium chemical plant. In 1954 Mutual
was acquired by the Allied Chemical Corporation, which eventually, in 1984, ceased operations in the Inner Harbor. As of
1987 the site was awaiting decontamination after the production there of toxic chromium compounds for more than 140
years.

*AUTOMOBILE: Soldiers Delight Natural Environment
Area is located northwest of Baltimore about 2.0 miles east
of Liberty Reservoir. The parking lot where this walk starts
is on Deer Park Road 2.3 miles north of the intersection
with Liberty Road.*

*From Interstate 695 (the Beltway) northwest of Balti-
more, take exit 18 for Route 26 west toward Randallstown.
Follow Route 26 (Liberty Road) about 5.0 miles to an intersection with Deer Park Road on the right near a large
water tower. Bear right onto Deer Park Road and go 2.3
miles to the Soldiers Delight parking lot on the left (or
west) side of the road.*

*WALK: As of 1987, the first route described below was
marked by orange blazes and the second route by green
blazes. The orange-blazed route lies on the east side of
Deer Park Road and the green-blazed trail on the west
side. Both walks start at the parking lot at the top of Berry
Hill on the west side of Deer Park Road, where in 1853
John Berry was gibbetted for the murder of his mother and
the attempted murder of his father.*

*Orange Trail—3.0 miles. From the south end of the
parking area, cross Deer Park Road and follow it south (or
right, relative to the way that you crossed the road from the
parking lot). Follow the edge of the road 60 yards to where
the trail veers left into the woods. Go 125 yards, then bear
left at an intersection of several trails. Bear left again in*

...ce to Isaac Tyson's Choate Mine.
...ath, passing another trail leading left.
..., turn right for 15 yards, then turn left
...eventually narrows to a footpath. Notice
...n vegetation as you head into an area of
a... ...il.

...t right at a four-way intersection of footpaths located 20 yards in front of a small clearing near a large garage. Continue through the woods to a field with a house on the right.

Head straight across the field and driveway and re-enter the woods. Pass a small pond (sometimes dry) about 20 yards to the right. Continue straight past minor side trails. Cross another clearing. Continue gradually downhill to a trail junction near Dolfield Road. Turn right and follow the path through the woods, across a stream, and gradually uphill through several clearings. Eventually, at a four-way trail intersection, you will cross the trail that you followed earlier.

Continue straight through the woods and across another clearing. Fork right at a trail junction. Follow the path gradually downhill through more open spaces, past a trail intersecting from the right, and back into the woods. Turn left uphill through more clearings. Continue straight gradually uphill. Turn left at the next trail junction, then turn right. Follow the path back to Deer Park Road, with the parking area to the left as you emerge from the woods.

Green Trail—2.0 miles. As noted earlier, a trail marked with green blazes forms a circuit on the west side of Deer Park Road. From the south end of the parking area, follow the road south 50 yards to where the footpath veers half-right into the woods. Follow the footpath for several hundred yards as it runs parallel to Deer Park Road before turning right onto a gravel road. Follow the gravel road through a picnic area and to the left past Red Dog Lodge. Fork left where the road splits in front of a large field visible in the distance behind some trees. Bear left again in a

*few dozen yards. Follow the rutted road around the field
and past the rubble of a small cellar hole. Continue toward
high electric transmission lines, passing (on your way toward the power lines) ruts intersecting from the right. Turn
right onto a rutted track directly under the power lines and
follow it downhill and then back to the crest of the hill below the stone lodge passed earlier. Continue under the
power lines to the bottom of the hill, then turn right to follow a footpath upstream along a brook. At first the brook is
to the right of the path, but eventually the trail crosses the
stream. At a fork in the trail, bear left back across the
stream. Follow the path uphill to Deer Park Road, with the
parking lot to your right as you emerge from the woods.*

Soldiers Delight is a state "natural environment area," meaning that aside from trails, no recreational development is
planned. The state first began to purchase land here in 1970
after ten years of lobbying and fund raising by local conservation groups, including the Citizens Committee for Soldiers Delight and Soldiers Delight Conservation, Inc. Money has been
supplied by private donations and the county, state, and federal
governments. About 2000 acres had been purchased as of
1987.

7

OREGON RIDGE

Walking and ski touring—3.0 miles (4.8 kilometers) round-trip. From Oregon Ridge Nature Center, hike to Ivy Hill Pond and back. The route crosses a wooded ridge on well-marked trails. The nature center building is open 9 AM to 5 PM daily, except Monday, Christmas, and New Year's Day. Call 771–0034 for information. The park is open daily from sunrise to sunset. Dogs must be leashed. Managed by the Baltimore County Department of Recreation and Parks (telephone 494–3817).

THE VIEW FROM OREGON RIDGE looks over the agricultural valleys of Oregon Branch and Western Run. To the north is Hayfields, long the estate of the Bosley and Merryman families, where in 1824 the Marquis de Lafayette visited Colonel Nicholas Merryman Bosley and presented him with a silver trophy from the Maryland Agricultural Society for the best cultivated Maryland farm. Immediately to the east is the Hunt Valley business community, since 1962 a major new source of nonagricultural employment. Farther north is Loveton Center, another new industrial complex (visible in the right-center of the photograph). Just beyond the fields in the center of the picture is Interstate 83, putting this attractive farm landscape within a half hour's drive of downtown Baltimore. Not surprisingly, in many places during recent years the fields of corn, barley, and soybeans have been replaced by new subdivisions and townhouse developments. In fact, Hayfields itself has been the subject of a series of development proposals since the early

1980s. Efforts to change the zoning to permit 1600 residential units at Hayfields were unsuccessful, but in 1986 the 474-acre farm was sold to another developer whose plans contemplate a golf course bordered by "estates" priced at $500,000 and more.

The patchwork quilt of farmland, subdivisions, and commercial development in the vicinity of Oregon Ridge epitomizes areas that are the subject of growing national concern about the loss of farmland. The concern is both aesthetic and economic. The conversion of farmland to scattered, low-density subdivisions (by far the most voracious use of land) not only chews up the countryside but also imposes on local governments an obligation to develop public services and capital improvements that typically cost much more than similar improvements for high-density housing—and more, too, than is generated in new tax revenues. Also, land that is easily developed for residential use because of level, deep, well-drained soils is for the same reasons excellent for crops. According to a Congressional report released in 1978, about one third of the several million acres of farm and pasture that are developed each year in the United States is prime agricultural land that will never again be used for producing food.

The rapid growth of suburban Baltimore, Washington, and other cities and towns has made Maryland a national leader in farmland loss, although not all of the decline is attributable to land development. When the suburban explosion began at the end of World War II, Maryland farms accounted for 4.2 million acres, or 67 percent of the state's total land. By 1980 farm acreage had dwindled to about 2.4 million acres, or 38 percent of the state's land area. By the year 2000 Maryland is expected to lose an additional 1 million acres of farmland, and all Marylanders presumably will pay the added transportation costs of importing still more produce from other states and countries.

Faced with the steady transformation of farms into suburbia, Maryland has developed a variety of programs intended to encourage the continued use of land for farming. In 1956 Maryland was the first state to enact a law (now 8–209 of the Tax-Property volume of the Annotated Code of Maryland) re-

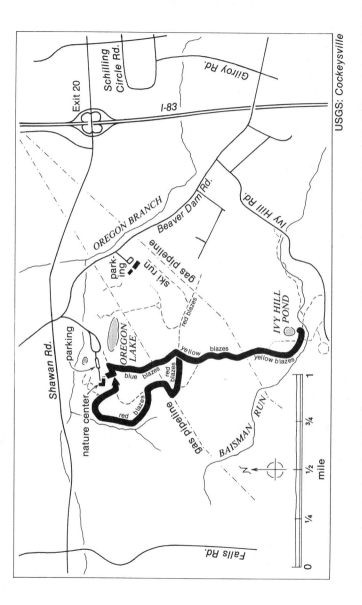

USGS: Cockeysville

quiring that farmland be assessed for property taxes not on the basis of its full development value but rather on the basis of its use for farming, as though that were all the land was good for. This preferential assessment was intended to provide staying power to farmers on the urban fringe, where higher taxes based on the land's enormous development potential were supposedly forcing farmers out of business (that is, causing them to sell their land for very substantial profits).

The remarkable thing about the preferential tax program, which with a few modifications has weathered a series of stormy attacks, is that landowners are required to give almost nothing in return. At most, an owner who sells or subdivides his farm property is simply required to pay an agricultural transfer tax equal to 5 percent of the sale price. As the result of various exceptions, the tax is usually less than that. Also, if the new owner signs a letter to the Department of Assessments and Taxation saying that he intends to farm the land for at least five more years, the sale does not trigger the transfer tax at all, and the land retains its preferential agricultural assessment until farming ceases or the land is sold again. Thus in Baltimore County, where the tax rate in 1987 was 3.06 percent and where a farm's agricultural assessment is often a small fraction of its normal assessment, only a few years are required for the transfer tax to be more than offset by the reduction in property taxes. And, of course, for anyone who holds land for a decade or more, the savings are enormous.

Equally remarkable is that despite the revenue loss of tens of millions of dollars annually suffered by the state and county treasuries, no evidence exists that the preferential assessment helps to preserve farmland. *Untaxing Open Space,* a 1976 report prepared for the federal government's Council on Environmental Quality, found that preferential assessment of agricultural land probably deters only 1 percent of all farmers from selling their land for development. Dr. Sidney Ishee of the University of Maryland, a longtime student of differential assessment in the state, has concluded that the law's principal effect is a temporary postponement of the development of farmland in some instances, but that the tax benefits are simply not strong enough to deter farmers near Baltimore and Washington from selling out at prices which in 1987 ranged up to ten or twenty times the farm-use value of the land. If common sense does not lead to this conclusion, a passing glance at the landscape does.

Some land use experts even argue that the preferential farm assessment encourages suburban sprawl. The artificially low taxes on farmland near cities enable owners to hold land off the market while prices climb higher still, with the result that development leapfrogs farther out. Even if preferential assessment does not encourage inefficient patterns of land development, there is little doubt that the tax break simply subsidizes speculators by reducing their holding costs, since any land that is farmed, regardless of ownership, qualifies for lower taxes. Land that has been sold to real estate syndicates at prices reflecting full development value continues to be assessed as though it were fit only for farming. For example, Hayfields, which was bought by a large developer in 1986 for $4.5 million, was assessed for tax purposes in 1987/88 at $225,880. Nor was an agricultural transfer tax collected; instead, Hayfield's new owner merely signed a letter stating that he intends to farm the land for at least five years, during which development plans for Hayfields are being formulated and discussed with local community groups and government officials.

Recognizing the ineffectiveness of preferential assessment to prevent the loss of farmland over the long term, the Maryland General Assembly has embarked on other efforts to obtain a more binding preservation commitment from farm owners. Of course, the usual way to gain permanent control over land is to buy it. But it is not necessary to buy the full interest in land— the so-called fee interest. Instead the state buys easements restricting development of the land. The term "easement" is somewhat misleading because these development right easements are *negative,* entailing nothing more than the extinguishment of the owner's right to develop his farmland to a more intensive use. The public is not granted right of access, as with an *affirmative* easement. Nor does purchase of the development rights enable the state to develop the land; it merely gives the state the enforceable right to prevent the landowner from doing so. And because the owner retains the right to farm his land just as he always has, acquisition of the development rights does not cost as much as purchase of the fee interest.

The preservation of farmland through the purchase of development right easements is one of the chief functions of the Maryland Agricultural Land Preservation Foundation, which was established in 1977 as an agency of the Maryland Department of Agriculture. As spelled out in 2–501 through 2–515 of the Agriculture volume of the Annotated Code of Maryland, the acquisition process begins with the filing of a petition by landowners to establish an agricultural preservation district. If the petition is approved by the local government and the Agricultural Land Preservation Foundation, landowners within the district must agree to maintain their land in agricultural use for at least five years. In return the local government must adopt an ordinance permitting and promoting agricultural activities within the district in order to protect farmers from nuisance suits and restrictive legislation filed by suburbanites who, for all their talk of the joys of country life, frequently are annoyed by the normal smells, sounds, and dust of farm operations. This protection for normal agricultural use is an important consideration in developing areas, where what some studies call an "impermanence syndrome" can develop among farmers who see land use patterns changing and farmers' political clout in local government overwhelmed by the tide of new suburban residents.

Once farmland is located within a preservation district, its owners may sell easements disposing of their development rights to the Agricultural Land Preservation Foundation. If the sale is approved, the purchase price is set by law as the difference between the value of the land with and without the bar on development (unless the owner's asking price is lower). A deed containing covenants that restrict the farmland to agricultural use is recorded among the county land records. The covenants are perpetual, although an owner can apply to buy the development rights back after twenty-five years or sooner if profitable farming is no longer feasible. If the resale is approved, the landowner must pay the then-market value of the development rights.

As of June 1987, more than 144,000 acres of farmland had been placed in 987 agricultural preservation districts, and easements restricting development had been acquired on 395 properties totaling about 60,000 acres, mostly in Baltimore, Carroll, Harford, Howard, and Montgomery counties. The easements typically cost between 30 and 40 percent of the market value of the land. In fiscal year 86/87, about $9 million was spent to acquire easements on more than 11,000 acres. Revenue to support this program comes from the state agricultural transfer tax (discussed earlier), from county matching funds, and from Program Open Space ($3 million in fiscal year 86/87).

An anomaly affecting the Agricultural Land Preservation Foundation is that a substantial added incentive to sell development rights would exist were it not for the present state of the law: because the sale of development rights reduces the value of the land, the property tax assessment should be reduced correspondingly, yet preferential farm assessment already grants all farmers this favored treatment even though they retain development rights.

Another state agency that is active in the preservation of farmland (as well as other undeveloped areas) is the Maryland Environmental Trust within the Department of Natural Resources. The Trust does not buy restrictive easements but merely acts as the recipient of donations by owners who share the Trust's goal of preserving scenic countryside and who welcome the substantial income tax deductions and estate tax savings that their donations produce. If the land has a substantial development potential, the charitable deduction resulting from a gift of the development rights to a governmental body can be very large—although the lowering of federal income tax rates starting in 1987 reduces the tax benefits of the charitable deduction. Also, of course, once the owner conveys the development rights, the fair market value of the property for estate and property tax purposes drops correspondingly. As of the beginning of 1987, the Maryland Environmental Trust held easements on 128 properties totaling 25,130 acres.

Because of the expense entailed in the purchase of development right easements and the understandable reluctance of most owners to give them away, some of the county governments are experimenting with a related approach designed to attract *private* money to the purchase of *transferable* development rights. For example, in Montgomery County a landowner in an agricultural district can sell his development rights to a developer who holds land in certain other designated development zones. Purchase of added development rights enables the developer to build residential units on his own land—not the farmer's land -- at a higher density than he would otherwise be permitted. This approach is supposed to help restrict farmland to farm use while at the same time promoting the more compact and efficient use of land in designated development zones, all at no cost to state or local governments. As of the beginning of 1986, $9 million worth of development rights for 2000 residential units had been transferred in Montgomery County in order to steer development away from a rural zone of 74,000 acres along the Potomac River.

Many counties are reluctant to rely on voluntary programs entailing compensation to landowners in order to restrict the development of farmland. Instead, local zoning ordinances attempt to discourage development in such areas by requiring large residential lots and various other limitations. For example, most of rural Howard County is zoned for lots of at least three acres, and parts of other counties are subject to a minimum development density of ten, twenty, and twenty-five acres per lot. In the past, however, large lot zoning has proven ineffective in preventing conversion of farmland to residential use. In fact, large lot zoning simply squanders farmland by forcing developers to use more land for fewer houses, which are then touted as "estates," "farmettes," and "executive home-sites" on the subdivision signs.

Some counties have gone a step farther than conventional large lot zoning by establishing agricultural preservation zones where farming is promoted and other land uses are severely restricted. For example, the Baltimore County Agricultural Preservation zone limits residential development to a maximum density of one house for each fifty acres.

In addition to state and local governments, various private conservation groups are active in the preservation of agricultural land and other scenic areas. Many of these groups, including the nationally active Nature Conservancy, the Chesapeake Bay Foundation, and the Conservation Trust of the Greenspring and Worthington valleys, themselves acquire restrictive easements and even fee interest in land. The Valleys Planning Council is a local group active in the preservation of land in north-central Baltimore County. Finally, the Oregon Ridge Nature Center Council (771–0034) focuses on land-use issues affecting properties in the vicinity of Oregon Ridge itself.

AUTOMOBILE: Oregon Ridge is located north of Baltimore near the Hunt Valley business community. The entrance is off Shawan Road 1.0 mile west of Interstate 83.

From Interstate 695 (the Beltway) north of Baltimore, take exit 24 for Interstate 83 north toward Timonium and York, Pa. Follow Interstate 83 north about 5.7 miles, then take exit 20B for Shawan Road west toward Oregon Ridge Park. Follow Shawan Road west about 1.0 mile, then turn left at a traffic light onto Beaver Dam Road. Go only 20 yards, then fork right toward the lake and the nature center. Follow the park road 0.4 mile to the nature center parking lot.

WALK: From the end of the parking lot, follow the asphalt road uphill to the Oregon Ridge Nature Center building.

After visiting the nature center, locate a pedestrian bridge leading from the end of the building across a ravine and into the woods. Cross the bridge and turn left downhill

at a T-intersection. Go 150 yards, then turn very sharply right uphill onto a trail marked with blue paint blazes. Follow the blue blazes uphill. Cross the wide swath of a gas pipeline right-of-way and continue uphill on the blue-blazed trail. The blue trail ends at a skewed four-way intersection.

From the end of the blue trail, cross a trail marked with red blazes, and follow the trail marked with yellow blazes. Continue on the wide yellow-blazed path through the woods, across another gas pipeline right-of-way, and downhill to the spillway from Ivy Hill Pond on the left (next to Baisman Run on the right).

Return from the pond the way you came. At the intersection of the yellow, red, and blue trails, turn sharply left onto the red-blazed trail. Follow the red blazes to a gas pipeline right-of-way. Turn right to follow the right-of-way 150 yards before veering left at the top of the hill; re-enter the woods on the red-blazed trail. Go 190 yards, then turn left to follow the red-blazed path downhill and along the side of a ravine, then eventually to the right. Continue straight past a memorial to Ann Franklin Ridgely. Go more or less straight on the wide, red-blazed trail where another path intersects from the rear-right. Continue to the bridge leading left across a ravine to the starting point at the nature center.

The "ravine" crossed by the bridge is actually one of the open pits or banks from which iron ore was dug for Oregon Furnace during the middle of the nineteenth century. Oregon Lake swimming pond (not to be confused with the pond below the nature center) is another ore bank, now flooded. There is a display on Oregon Furnace in the nature center building.

8

GUNPOWDER FALLS STATE PARK

West Hereford

Walking—6.5 miles (10.5 kilometers) round-trip. Well-marked footpaths wind along the valley slopes, ridge tops, and river bank bordering Big Gunpowder Falls. From the Bunker Hill park entrance, follow the rocky gorge to Pretty-boy Dam and back. The trails are sometimes rugged and the circuit rather strenuous. The park is open daily from sunrise to sunset. Dogs must be leashed. Managed by the Maryland Park Service (telephone 592–2897).

LONG STRETCHES OF BIG and Little Gunpowder Falls have been developed into a linear valley park. Most of the park follows Big Gunpowder Falls diagonally across Baltimore County from northwest to southeast—from just below Pretty-boy Reservoir to the river's mouth at Chesapeake Bay. Another arm follows the roughly parallel course of Little Gunpowder Falls, which forms the boundary between Baltimore and Harford counties. Some sections of the park, notably at Hereford, now provide an outstanding opportunity for walking in a rocky and wild setting.

Compared to Baltimore City's basic park system, which was created about the turn of the century, Gunpowder Falls State Park is relatively new, having been planned and acquired in response to the rapid suburbanization of Baltimore County after World War II. Since 1958, when the Maryland State Planning Commission first recommended a system of unconnected parks

along both branches of Gunpowder Falls, the Maryland General Assembly has authorized acquisition of 15,646 acres, of which more than 85 percent had been purchased by the beginning of 1987.

Just how does the state go about actually acquiring this (or any) parkland? It is a painstaking and sometimes painful process. In the case of Gunpowder Falls State Park, most owners, particularly owners of vacant, unproductive land along the two valleys, have been amenable to selling, but some unhappiness is inevitable when the state sets out to buy about three dozen homes and more than 15,000 acres (4000 acres in the Hereford area alone).

Price, of course, is the principal issue. To protect the interests of both the property owner and the state, the Department of General Services, the agency that handles land acquisition for Maryland's parks, is required to hire two independent appraisers to make separate determinations of fair market value of each property. The appraisals are reviewed by the Department's staff and if one or the other is approved, an offer in that amount is made to the owner. Sometimes a third appraisal is necessary if the first two figures are far apart, for the evaluation of real estate is not a precise technique. Occasionally an owner will obtain yet another appraisal which may convince the state's reviewers and the Board of Public Works (which must approve all acquisitions) that a higher price is in fact justified.

If a price cannot be agreed upon, the Department of General Services in consultation with the Department of Natural Resources may simply wait in order to try again later with a new appraisal and offer. Or the matter may be turned over to the Attorney General's Office for condemnation, so that eventually the value of the property is decided by a jury unless the case is first settled by agreement. If the state declines to pay the amount set by the jury and instead abandons the acquisition, the owner's legal costs are paid by the state.

The procedural safeguards of appraisal and condemnation are intended, of course, to provide a neutral determination of fair market value. For some properties, however, a price may

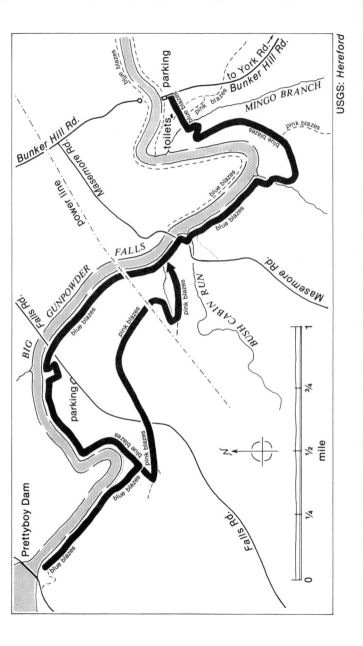

USGS: *Hereford*

be *fair* but nonetheless *inadequate*. For example, if forced to sell for fair market value, the owner of an unusually small or dilapidated or substandard house could not today buy another home in his community for what his own is worth. The result is a dilemma that, for a period, was an impasse in the acquisition of some such properties for Gunpowder Falls State Park. In 1979, however, when the Gunpowder project began to receive federal funds, the payment of relocation assistance became mandatory under federal law. As of 1987, payments of up to $15,000 (in addition to the agreed acquisition price) were authorized to help displaced homeowners buy comparable houses nearby that are also "decent, safe and sanitary." In exceptional cases even greater assistance is available. Also, state aid has long been available to cover actual moving costs.

For some owners, however, the problem has not been price but preference: a simple desire to stay where they are. These cases have dragged on for years until only the most difficult are left, often involving holdings entirely surrounded by park property or wedges of private ownership penetrating deep into the park. In some cases the Department of General Services has tried to reach a variety of arrangements with people who do not want to move from their homes or established businesses. Elderly owners are commonly offered a life license under which the state acquires the property outright for its full value while the former owners retain the privilege to occupy the house for the rest of their lives. They maintain and insure the property but pay no taxes or rent. Another option is a life estate, which requires that the purchase price be reduced by the value of the sellers' right of continued occupancy, as estimated by their life expectancy. Owners of the life estate continue to pay property taxes. In a few cases the state has bought the property and then leased it back to the former owners, an arrangement that has been attractive to farmers who are approaching retirement but want to continue to farm their land for a few more years.

Around the perimeter of the park, the state has had trouble buying parts of individual holdings needed to form a readily identifiable boundary that bears an intelligent relationship to the topography of the area and to local roads. Owners have complained that their "back yards" are being taken—that is, tracts stretching hundreds of feet into the woods behind their houses. With these owners, the Department of General Services is experimenting with a variety of affirmative and negative easements. The former allows certain public uses of the land and the latter prohibits development or logging. All of these techniques not only ease the acquisition process but also reduce the state's purchase expenses and maintenance costs.

Finally, a word about where the money for the acquisition and development of Maryland's state parks comes from. Since 1969 the principal source has been Program Open Space, funded by a share of the state tax of 0.5 percent on real estate transactions. The only other source has been federal assistance from the Land and Water Conservation Fund, which is financed largely by revenues from offshore oil and gas leases. The Land and Water Conservation Fund was established in 1965, but its grants to the states have been greatly curtailed since 1981. To compensate for this loss, the pace of spending by Maryland must be increased if the state hopes to win the race with land developers and to acquire all of the areas at Gunpowder Falls and other state parks recommended by park planners.

To speed up the acquisition of parkland, the Maryland General Assembly did, in fact, enact legislation in 1987 to increase Program Open Space's share of revenues from the state transfer tax, and also to extend the duration of Program Open Space beyond its scheduled expiration in 1990. Conservationists have applauded these measures, but they also point out that as originally enacted in 1969, all state transfer tax revenues went to Program Open Space. In 1984, however, the legislature and governor agreed to start diverting huge sums—more than half the transfer tax revenues—from Program Open Space to the state's general fund. Since then the responsibilities of Program Open Space have been greatly expanded to include not only park acquisition, but also the preservation of agricultural land (as discussed in Chapter 7) and other state and local programs that cannot possibly be funded adequately unless the state transfer tax on real estate is again allocated exclusively to Program Open Space.

AUTOMOBILE: The section of Gunpowder Falls State Park explored by this walk is located north of Baltimore near Prettyboy Reservoir. Park at the end of Bunker Hill Road, which is reached from York Road in Hereford.

From Interstate 695 (the Beltway) north of Baltimore, take exit 24 for Interstate 83 north toward Timonium and York, Pa. Follow Interstate 83 north 12.4 miles, then take exit 27 for Route 137 (Mt. Carmel Road) and Hereford. At the top of the exit ramp, turn right (east) onto Route 137 and go 0.4 mile to a T-intersection with Route 45 (York Road). Turn left (north) onto Route 45 and go 0.8 mile to an intersection with Bunker Hill Road on the left. Turn left onto Bunker Hill Road and follow it 1.1 miles to the large parking lot next to Big Gunpowder Falls. (There are no falls as such; for a discussion of the word "falls," see Chapter 9.)

WALK: Start at the parking lot where Bunker Hill Road meets the river. A pedestrian bridge over the river is planned for this location. If it has been built, you may want to return at the end of your walk along the north bank of the river, as noted below at the appropriate point in the directions; but look now to see if the bridge is there.

The walk starts where Bunker Hill Road enters the parking lot. Locate Gunpowder South Trail, which is blazed with blue dots and crosses the road a few yards uphill from the parking lot. The route described here follows the blue-dot trail all the way to Prettyboy Dam.

With your back to the river and the parking lot, turn right off Bunker Hill Road and follow blue-blazed Gunpowder South Trail obliquely uphill and straight through a stand of pines at the top of the slope. Cross the Bunker Hill Trail (pink dots) and continue straight downhill on the

blue-blazed trail. Cross a stream (Mingo Branch) and turn left. Zigzag uphill, then continue along the top of the ridge between the valley of Mingo Branch on the left and the valley of Big Gunpowder Falls on the right. Pass a trail junction where Mingo Forks Trail (pink dots) intersects from the left. Continue downhill on the blue-blazed trail and along a ravine. Cross a stream and continue on the blue-blazed trail to the edge of Big Gunpowder Falls. With the river on your right, follow the blue-blazed path upstream. Be alert for places where the path is eroding into the stream. Just before reaching Masemore Road, fork right to cross Bush Cabin Run on stepping stones (but do not cross if the water is flowing over the stones).

From the south (or near) end of the Masemore Road bridge, continue upstream with the river on your right. Fork right to continue along the river and across a small stream. Follow the riverside path upstream to Falls Road.

Cross Falls Road and continue upstream with the river on your right. After only 90 yards, detour left uphill to bypass a large rock formation; climb to the left for 20 yards, then bear left again on the blue-dot trail. (Give wide berth to any snakes sunning themselves on the rocks; some people claim to have seen copperheads in this area.)

After climbing far above the rock formation, descend to the river's edge. With the river on your right, continue upstream. Pass through a long area of jumbled rocks where the path is very obscure; simply continue upstream. Eventually, as the valley bends sharply left, the riverside path becomes smoother. Then, as the valley begins to turn right, fork left uphill on the blue-blazed trail. Follow the blue dots obliquely uphill to the intersection with the Highland Trail (pink dots). You will take this trail on the return leg. For now, however, turn right downhill on the blue-dot trail. Follow the side of the valley, then the river's edge, upstream to the base of Prettyboy Dam. If you want to, you can climb to the top of the dam on a trail starting by the

*river opposite a large, flat rock about 100 yards below
the dam.*

*From the base of Prettyboy Dam, return downstream
with the river on your left, then climb half-right away from
the river to the intersection with Highland Trail that you
passed earlier. Turn right to leave blue-blazed Gunpowder
South Trail and follow instead pink-blazed Highland Trail
uphill. At a T-intersection, turn left and follow the ridge
uphill to Falls Road.*

*Cross Falls Road and continue on a path opposite. Pass
green steel posts. (A parking lot may be built here, and
also a new trail leading downhill to the river.) Continue
straight through the woods on the pink-dot trail. Cross a
right-of-way under high electric transmission lines and re-
enter the woods on the footpath blazed with pink dots. Descend to a stream and follow it upstream. Cross the stream
just short of the power line right-of-way. Turn left and
climb to an intersection with a wide path. Bear left and follow the path gradually downhill to Gunpowder South Trail
(blue dots) next to the river. With the river on your left,
bear right downstream and continue to Masemore Road.*

*If the pedestrian bridge at Bunker Hill has been built,
cross the Masemore Road bridge and turn right downstream on the riverside path that leads to Bunker Hill
Road. Otherwise, follow Masemore Road right for 60
yards to pick up the blue-dot trail where it crosses Bush
Cabin Run on stepping stones a few yards from the end of
the guardrail at the parking area. This is the trail that you
took earlier from Bunker Hill. Follow it back to your starting point.*

9

GUNPOWDER FALLS STATE PARK

East Hereford

Walking—4.0 miles (6.4 kilometers). Follow a well-marked footpath from York Road downstream along a wild and winding stretch of river to Panther Branch. Return through woods and farmland above the valley. The park is open daily from sunrise to sunset. Dogs must be leashed. Managed by the Maryland Park Service (telephone 592–2897).

IN COMMON PARLANCE in these parts, Baltimore is "Bawlamer." A brief lexicon of other Bawlamer locutions, such as "Merlin" for Maryland, "Naplis" for our state capital, "Anna Runnel" and "Harrid" for two of our nearby counties, and "Droodle" for Druid Hill, is contained in the urban guidebook *Bawlamer,* published by the Citizens Housing and Planning Association. Less well-known, however, is that our Baltimore dialect is marked by other geographic expressions that are peculiar not for pronunciation but for usage.

Heading the list is *falls,* as in Big Gunpowder Falls. The focus of the present chapter, of course, is not a local Niagara or even a waterfall at all. Indeed, during dry periods or at other times when water is not being released from Prettyboy Reservoir or Loch Raven, the Gunpowder not only does not *fall* but scarcely even *flows.*

According to William B. Mayre, a Maryland historian who made a specialty of place names, court records, and old documents of every variety, Baltimore County and its environs are

the only area in the United States where there are whole freshwater rivers and streams called *falls*. Apparently early settlers along the tidal shores of the Gunpowder River and the Patapsco River (or rather "Patapsico," in our local patois) called the swift and rocky freshwater streams above tidewater the *falls* of those rivers. Hence Big Gunpowder Falls and, for the smaller stream to the north, Little Gunpowder Falls, both of which empty into the tidal Gunpowder River. Jones Falls is the freshwater portion of the Northwest Branch of the Patapsco River. Gwynns Falls is the falls of the Middle Branch. Similarly, old maps and other documents call the main branch of the Patapsco that flows through the state park Patapsco *Falls*. An early nineteenth-century print in the possession of the Maryland Historical Society depicts the original mill at Oella and states on its face: "Union Manufactories of Maryland on Patapsco Falls, Baltimore County."

If a major freshwater stream of the Baltimore Piedmont is a *falls*, a middling stream is a *run* and a minor one is a *branch*. Hence in Baltimore we have Charles Run, Dead Run, Western Run, Stony Run, Chinquapin Run, Herring Run, and Moores Run. As noted in the last chapter, two of the tributary runs and branches feeding Big Gunpowder Falls are Bush Cabin Run and Mingo Branch, and the present walk passes Panther Branch.

With the exception of the various tidal arms of Baltimore Harbor, the saltwater counterpart to a tributary run or branch is a *creek*, unless the saltwater appendage is so small and serpentine as to be a *gut*. Thus, off the north side of the Patapsco River we have in rapid succession North Point Creek, Shallow Creek, Bear Creek, and Colgate Creek. In the Baltimore region there are only a few exceptions (notably Deer Creek) to the reservation of *creek* for a small tidal river. And off the creeks branch myriad *coves*.

Finally, perhaps you are wondering about brook. Mr. Mayre dismisses the term as "literary." It is virtually never seen in old deeds or other documents and appears only in the contrived

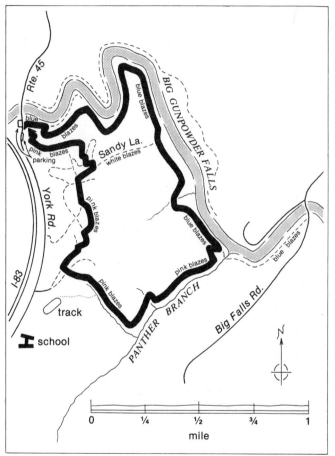

USGS: *Hereford*

names given to housing subdivisions and suburban cul-de-sacs.

So much for *falls* and other riverine terms, but what about "Gunpowder"? The name occurs not only in Big and Little Gunpowder Falls but also in Gunpowder Neck and Gunpowder Island (now Carroll Island). Although most accounts assume that the name originated with gunpowder mills, *The Traveller's Directory,* or *A Pocket Companion to the Philadelphia-Baltimore Road,* published in 1802, gives the following explanation:

> Great Gunpowder River—Between this and Bush River is Gunpowder Neck, so named from a tradition that the Indians, who formerly lived in this tract, when first acquainted with the use of gunpowder, supposed it to be a vegetable seed; they purchased a quantity and sowed it on this neck, expecting it to produce a good crop.

AUTOMOBILE: The section of Gunpowder Falls State Park explored by this walk is located north of Baltimore a few miles east of Prettyboy Reservoir. Park your car on York Road 1.7 miles north of Hereford.

From Interstate 695 (the Beltway) north of Baltimore, take exit 24 for Interstate 83 north toward Timonium and York, Pa. Follow Interstate 83 north 12.4 miles, then take exit 27 for Route 137 (Mt. Carmel Road) and Hereford. At the top of the exit ramp, turn right (east) onto Route 137 and go 0.4 mile to a T-intersection with Route 45 (York Road). Turn left onto Route 45 and go 1.7 miles. Just before the road crosses the bridge over Big Gunpowder Falls, park in one of the small lots on either side of the road.

WALK: The walk starts from the meadow east (or downstream) from York Road. Pick up the trail where it crosses a small stream about 40 yards from the river's edge. Nearby is a stone fireplace. Fork left onto the Gunpowder South Trail, which is blazed with blue dots. You will return later by the other fork (that is, by the Panther Branch Trail, blazed with pink dots).

Follow blue-dotted Gunpowder South Trail through the brush to the river's edge. In a few dozen yards, fork right uphill away from the river on the blue-blazed trail. Zigzag uphill along the side of the valley. Continue along the crest of the slope, then descend to the bottom of the valley.

With the river on your left, follow the path downstream, usually near the water but sometimes farther up the side of the valley. Be alert for places where the path is eroding into the river. After about a mile, turn left at a trail intersection with Sandy Lane Trail (white dots).

Continue to follow blue-blazed Gunpowder South Trail through the woods and along the foot of the bluff at a distance from the river. Eventually, follow the path to the right up a ravine, across a stream, then up and to the left above the river. With the river downhill on your left, continue along the side of the valley. Descend gradually to the river's edge and continue downstream.

Twenty yards before a stream (Panther Branch) joins the river from the right, turn very sharply right onto the Panther Branch Trail, a narrow footpath blazed with pink dots. The trail zigzags uphill over a shoulder and down to the right. For the rest of the walk, follow the pink dots of the Panther Branch Trail. As you will see if you have sharp eyes, the ravine at Panther Branch contains some old stone foundations that may be the ruins of a gristmill and its companion gunpowder mill that blew up on July 7, 1874.

With Panther Branch on your left, follow the pink-dot path up a ravine. Eventually, climb to the right (look for traces of an old millrace on the right) and follow a smaller ravine for a short distance before turning left to cross a rivulet. Continue above Panther Branch. Bear right again up another side ravine. With a very small stream on your left, follow the pink dots up the ravine and past several paths intersecting from the left Follow the pink dots to a weedy field dotted with scrub at the head of the ravine. Bear half-left uphill and then straight across a cultivated field. Cross a rutted road, then immediately turn right onto a grassy

track. Continue with a pine plantation on your left and a hedgerow (and field beyond) on your right.

Follow the track into the woods, still with a pine planta-tion on your left. Jog left, then right, and continue through deciduous woods. Sixty yards after the path turns downhill to the left, leave the dirt road and turn right on the pink-dot footpath. Follow the pink dots downhill through the woods. Emerge into a clearing and climb obliquely to a grassy path in front of another pine plantation. Follow the path right. Continue straight through a grassy crossroads, then turn right in 15 yards at a trail intersection by the cor-ner of a pine plantation. Follow the pink dots as the trail veers left at the next intersection (instead of proceeding straight downhill on Sandy Lane Trail). Turn left again im-mediately on a narrow footpath through the woods (instead of proceeding straight downhill on the fire lane around the edge of the pines). Follow the footpath for 50 yards, then turn right. Go 30 yards, then bear left onto a narrow foot-path. Follow the pink dots down a ravine, across a gully, along the side of the valley, and back to the meadow by York Road and Big Gunpowder Falls.

10

GUNPOWDER FALLS STATE PARK

Northern Central Railroad Trail

Walking, bicycling, and ski touring—up to 20.0 miles (32.2 kilometers) one way. Walk from Ashland north to the Pennsylvania line (or vice versa) along an old railroad that now forms a hiker's highway through forest and farmland. The rails and ties have been removed and the roadbed cleared of brush, so that the entire trail is passable on foot. Between Ashland and Monkton the trail has been paved with finely crushed stone, and so is suitable for bicyclists also. Note, however, that north of Monkton a few of the bridges, although passable, are not in good condition; they may lack railings or have holes in their beds, so be cautious while crossing bridges. Also, the roadbed has been damaged by erosion in a few places. If you do not want to retrace your steps, a car shuttle is necessary. Aside from Ashland and the Pennylvania line, two other access points are described under the automobile directions, making possible several shorter trips. The trail is open daily from sunrise to sunset. Dogs must be leashed. Managed by the Maryland Park Service (telephone 592–2897).

HIKE TO PENNSYLVANIA. From Ashland near Cockeysville, a hiker/biker trail follows the old roadbed of the Northern Central Railroad for 20 miles north to the Mason-Dixon line, where the trail abruptly ends because Pennsylvania has not moved as quickly as Maryland to refurbish the railroad for rec-

reational use. If I may editorialize for a moment, writing my various *Country Walks* books has made me familiar with a number of Rails-to-Trails projects, and this is the best I have ever seen. For mile after mile the trail follows the banks of Big Gunpowder Falls, Little Falls, and Beetree Run across Maryland's rolling Piedmont landscape, passing through Glencoe, Corbett, Monkton, White Hall, Parkton, and other small towns along the way.

The Northern Central Railroad was founded as the Baltimore & Susquehanna in 1828, shortly after the creation of the Baltimore & Ohio Railroad. Chronically undercapitalized, the B&S took ten years to construct its line as far as York, Pennsylvania. Not until 1851 (the same year that the B&O completed its line to Wheeling, West Virginia) did the B&S reach the vicinity of Harrisburg, where there was a junction with the east-west line of the Pennsylvania Railroad. By that time the state of Maryland was virtual owner of the Baltimore & Susquehanna, which had received state loans and a forbearance of interest payments altogether totaling $3 million. Private shareholders and Baltimore City, which expected to benefit from the line, had a stake totaling only $1.2 million.

In 1854 the Baltimore & Susquehanna merged with two other railroads, and the combined enterprise was named the Northern Central Railway. By then the Pennsylvania Railroad linked Philadelphia and Pittsburgh, enhancing the value of the Northern Central. From the Harrisburg junction, the Northern Central provided a shorter route to tidewater than did the Pennsylvania Railroad's main trunk line to Philadelphia.

During the 1850s the Baltimore & Ohio Railroad sought to gain control over the Northern Central—or at least to prevent others from doing so—by buying up a large part of its shares, but in 1860 the B&O let down its guard and sold its Northern Central stock. The Pennsylvania Railroad, chief competitor of the B&O, then purchased a controlling interest in the Northern Central, and thus gained access to Baltimore's market and port.

During the Civil War the Northern Central was repeatedly a target of saboteurs and Confederate raiders. On the day after

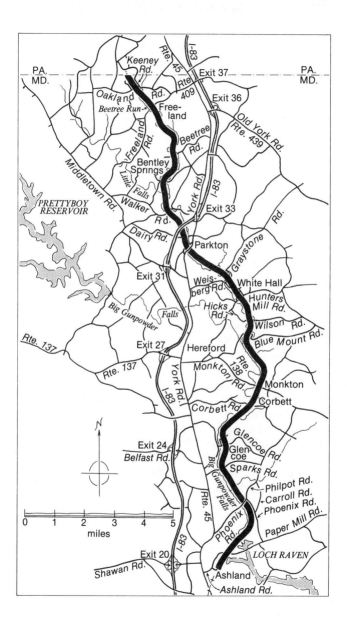

the confrontation of April 19, 1861, between a Baltimore mob and the Sixth Massachusetts Regiment on its way to Washington, Mayor Brown and Governor Hicks authorized burning the railroad bridges leading from the north into Baltimore in order to prevent the arrival of more federal troops and the outbreak of more rioting. As reported in the newspapers, a party of cheering and shouting Southern sympathizers destroyed two Northern Central bridges near Cockeysville and several more closer to Baltimore, as well as some B&O bridges. The spans were rebuilt, but in 1863 other Northern Central bridges were wrecked during Robert E. Lee's invasion culminating at Gettysburg. Again in 1864 the Cockeysville bridges were burned by Colonel Harry Gilmor's Confederate raiders during Jubal Early's march through Maryland.

Following the Civil War, the Northern Central was operated as an adjunct to the Pennsylvania Railroad, which in 1874 absorbed the Northern Central Railway Company and in 1900 leased its right-of-way for 999 years. Served by both the Baltimore & Ohio and the Pennsylvania Railroad, Baltimore became a major center for the export of grain, which before 1870 came mainly from nearby states but thereafter mostly from the Midwest. The Northern Central also carried farm produce and other freight south from Harrisburg, York, and a number of agricultural towns and factory complexes in northern Baltimore County.

People who knew the Northern Central as a working railroad remember it chiefly as a commuter line from Parkton southward into Baltimore's old Calvert Street station, a site now occupied by the Sunpapers building. Termed collectively the Parkton Local (or sometimes the Ruxton Rocket), the commuter trains were running only three times daily by the late 1950s. Commenting on the trains' arrival downtown at 7:30, 8:30, and 10 AM, Ralph Reppert of the Sunpapers said that the schedule accommodated "the workers, the clerkers, and the shirkers." After complaining for decades of its losses on the Northern Central line, the Pennsylvania Railroad was allowed to terminate local passenger service on June 27, 1959. Long-distance passenger service over the Northern Central line ended in 1971. Finally, freight service was halted abruptly and permanently—at least for the section north of Cockeysville—when the railroad was severely damaged by flooding from Tropical Storm Agnes in 1972. Having declared bankruptcy in 1970, the Pennsylvania Railroad refused to repair the Northern Central north of Cockeysville. The abandoned line was eventually purchased from the Penn Central Corporation and the Northern Central Railroad Company by the state of Maryland in 1980, two years after the U.S. Department of the Interior had approved a Rails-to-Trails grant to the state of $450,000.

Although the Northern Central line from Ashland northward is now a hiker/biker trail, there is still talk of rehabilitating the right-of-way south of Cockeysville for use by light-rail commuter trains.

AUTOMOBILE: The Northern Central Railroad Trail is located north of Baltimore. The four access points described below are easily reached from various exits off Interstate 83. If you do not want to retrace your steps, a car shuttle is necessary. Obviously, a shuttle involves either two cars and two driver-hikers, or a driver who drops you off at the start (after you have left your car at the end) or who simply meets you at the end. This is what friends and family are for. In any case, as shown on the map, Interstate 83 and York Road (which run more or less parallel to each other) provide good linkage for shuttling cars between the access points described here.

Ashland *is located at the southern end of the Northern Central Railroad Trail. From Interstate 695 (the Beltway) north of Baltimore, take exit 24 for Interstate 83 north toward Timonium and York, Pa. Follow Interstate 83 north 5.5 miles, then take exit 20A for Shawan Road east toward Cockeysville. Follow Shawan Road 0.7 mile, then turn right (south) at a T-intersection with Route 45 (York Road). Follow Route 45 south 0.3 mile, then turn left onto Ashland Road (toward Papermill Road). Go 0.4 mile, then head* half-right on Ashland Road into a housing development called Ashland at Hunt Valley. Continue straight on Ashland Road for 0.25 mile to a parking lot for Gunpowder Falls State Park—Northern Central Railroad Trail. Ashland, incidentally, was once an iron-making community, and the long stone building to the left of the parking lot incorporates former tenant housing.

Monkton is located 7.5 miles north of Ashland and 5.4 miles south of Parkton on the railroad trail. From Interstate 83 about 12.4 miles north of the Beltway, take exit 27 for Route 137 (Mt. Carmel Road) and Hereford. At the top of the exit ramp, turn right (east) onto Route 137 and go 0.4 mile, then turn right (south) at a T-intersection with Route 45 (York Road). Follow Route 45 south 100 yards, then turn left onto Route 138 (Monkton Road). Follow Route 138 for about 3.0 miles, then (after crossing Big Gunpowder Falls) turn left into a parking lot for Gunpowder Falls State Park—Northern Central Railroad Trail. The lot is located opposite an intersection with Old Monkton Road.

Parkton is located 5.4 miles north of Monkton and 7.0 miles south of the Maryland-Pennsylvania boundary on the railroad trail. From Interstate 83 about 15.8 miles north of the Beltway, take exit 31 for Middletown Road and Parkton. From the top of the exit ramp, turn right (east) and follow Middletown Road 0.6 mile, then turn left (north) at a T-intersection with Route 45 (York Road). Follow Route 45 north 1.2 miles, then turn very sharply left onto the former York Road (now a dead end). Follow the former York Road 0.1 mile across a stone bridge. Park on the left at the end of the road next to Gunpowder Falls State Park—Northern Central Railroad Trail.

The boundary between Maryland and Pennsylvania (which as of 1987 was the northern end of the railroad trail) is located 7.0 miles north of Parkton. From Interstate 83 about 21.7 miles north of the Beltway, take exit 36 for Route 439, Maryland Line and Bel Air. From the top of the *exit ramp, turn right (west) to follow Route 439 toward Maryland Line. Go 0.3 mile, then turn right (north) onto Route 45 (York Road). Follow Route 45 north 1.0 mile to a crossroads with Route 409 (Freeland Road). Turn left (west) onto Route 409 and go 0.9 mile, then turn right onto Oakland Road. Go 1.5 miles as Oakland Road winds over hill and dale, then turn left under the railroad in order to continue on Oakland Road where Keeney Road goes straight. Immediately after passing under the railroad, turn right onto a dead end road. Go 100 yards, then park on the right—that is, on the old railroad bed itself. The Maryland-Pennsylvania boundary is located a few minutes walk to the north or away from the Oakland Road under-pass.*

WALK: From the parking lot in Ashland, there is only one way to go on the railroad trail—north. The route is un-mistakable all the way through Monkton and Parkton to the Pennsylvania line. However, it is occasionally necessary to cross or follow roads for short distances. In such cases, use caution; if you must walk along a road, follow the left shoulder in order to minimize the risk of being hit by a car approaching from behind.

From Monkton or Parkton, you can walk north or south.

Finally, from the parking area near the Maryland-Pennsylvania line, the state boundary is located a few hun-dred yards to the north, and presumably you will want to end (or start) your walk at the actual Mason-Dixon line.

11

ROBERT E. LEE PARK

Lake Roland

*Walking—5.5 miles (8.9 kilometers) round-trip. An easy foot-
path borders Lake Roland and its tributary streams. Walk
from the dam at the lake's southern end to the marsh and
meadow at the northern end, then return the way you came.
The park is open daily from sunrise to sunset. Dogs must be
leashed. Managed by the Baltimore City Department of Recreation and Parks (telephone 396–6106).*

BECAUSE OF THE VARIETY of its habitats—bottomland
woods, meadows, freshwater marsh, dry piney highlands, and
open water—Robert E. Lee Park (Lake Roland) is particularly
popular with birdwatchers, although most of the areas described in this book, even those well within the city, are also
good for birding.

About 650 species of birds live and breed in the United
States and Canada, but many of these are not found east of the
Rocky Mountains. The 1986 edition of the *Field Checklist of
Maryland & D.C. Birds,* copublished by the Maryland Orni-
thological Society and the Audubon Naturalist Society of the
Central Atlantic states, lists 311 regularly occurring species.
Another seventy are "rarities and accidentals" in our area.

Even for fledgling birders, identifying the many species that
nest in the Baltimore area or pass through during migration is
easier than might at first be thought. Shape, size, plumage, and
other physical characteristics are distinguishing field marks.

Range, season, habitat, song, and behavior are other useful keys to identifying birds.

Range is of primary importance for the simple reason that many birds are not found throughout North America or even the eastern United States, but only in certain regions such as the Atlantic and Gulf coasts. For example, cedar waxwings and Bohemian waxwings closely resemble each other, so it helps to know that the latter are not seen in Maryland. A good field guide provides range maps based on years of reported sightings and bird counts. Of course, bird ranges are not static: some pioneering species, such as the glossy ibis and house finch, have extended their ranges during recent decades. Other birds, such as the ivory-billed woodpecker, have lost ground and may even have died out.

Season is related to range, since migratory birds appear in different parts of their ranges during different times of year. The five species of spot-breasted thrushes, for instance, are sometimes difficult to distinguish from each other, but usually only the hermit thrush is present in eastern Maryland during winter and only the wood thrush is found here during summer. Again, the maps in most field guides reflect this sort of information.

Habitat is important in identifying birds. Even before you spot a bird, the surroundings can tell you what species you are likely to see. Within its range a species usually appears only in certain preferred habitats, although during migration some species are less particular. (In many cases, birds show a degree of physical adaptation to their preferred environment.) As its name implies, the marsh wren is seldom found far from cat-tails, rushes, sedges, or tall marsh grasses; if a wrenlike bird is spotted in such a setting, it is unlikely to be a house wren or Carolina wren or one of the other species commonly found in thick underbrush or shrubbery. Ducks can be difficult to identify unless you tote a telescope; but even if all you can see is a silhouette, you can start with the knowledge that shallow marshes and creeks normally attract few diving ducks (such as oldsquaw, canvasbacks, redheads, ring-necked ducks, greater

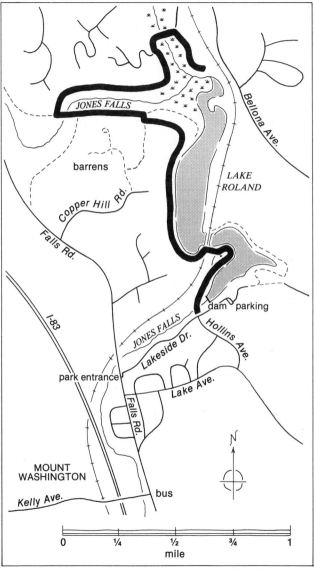

JONES FALLS

barrens

Copper Hill Rd.

Falls Rd.

I-83

park entrance

Falls Rd.

MOUNT
WASHINGTON

Kelly Ave.

bus

LAKE
ROLAND

Bellona Ave.

dam parking

Jones Falls

Lakeside Dr.

Hollins Ave.

Lake Ave.

N

0   ¼   ½   ¾   1
mile

USGS: *Cockeysville*

and lesser scaup, common goldeneye, and buffleheads) and that large, deep bodies of water are not the usual setting for surface-feeding puddle ducks (American black ducks, gadwalls, mallards, common pintails, American widgeons, wood ducks, northern shovelers, and blue-winged and green-winged teals).

Some of the distinctive habitats that different bird species prefer are open ocean; beaches; salt marsh; mud flats; meadows; thickets; various types of woods; and creeks, ponds, and lakes. The area where two habitats join, called an *ecotone,* is a particularly good place to look for birds because species peculiar to either environment might be present. For example, both meadowlarks and wood warblers might be found where a hay field abuts a forest. All good field guides provide information on habitat preferences that can help to locate a species or to assess the likelihood of a tentative identification.

Song announces the identity (or at least the location) of birds even before they are seen. Although some species, such as the red-winged blackbird, have only a few songs, others, such as the mockingbird, have an infinite variety. Some birds, most notably thrushes, sing different songs in the morning and evening. In many species the basic songs vary among individuals and also from one area to another, giving rise to regional "dialects." Nonetheless, the vocal repertory of most songbirds is sufficiently constant in timbre and pattern to identify each species simply by its songs.

Bird songs, as distinguished from calls, can be very complex. They are sung only by the male of most species, usually in spring and summer. The male arrives first at the breeding and nesting area after migration. He stakes out a territory for courting, mating, and nesting by singing at prominent points around the area's perimeter. This wards off intrusion by other males of his species and simultaneously attracts females. On the basis of the male's display or the desirability of his territory, the female selects her mate. Experiments suggests that female birds build nests faster and lay more eggs when exposed to the songs of males with a larger vocal repertory than others of their species, and the relative volume of their songs appears to be a way for males to establish status among themselves.

In a few species, including eastern bluebirds, "Baltimore" orioles, cardinals, and white-throated sparrows, both sexes sing, although the males are more active in defending their breeding territory. Among mockingbirds, both sexes sing in fall and winter, but only males sing in spring and summer. Some birds, such as canaries, have different songs for different seasons.

Birds tend to heed the songs of their own kind and to ignore the songs of other species, which do not compete for females nor, in many cases, for the same type of nesting materials or food. In consequence, a single area might include the overlapping breeding territories of several species. From year to year such territories are bigger or smaller, depending on the food supply. Typically, most small songbirds require about half an acre from which others of their species are excluded.

Bird calls (as distinguished from songs) are short, simple, sometimes harsh, and used by both males and females at all times of year to communicate alarm, aggression, location, and existence of food. Nearly all birds have some form of call. Warning calls are often heeded by species other than the caller's. Some warning calls are thin, high-pitched whistles that are difficult to locate and so do not reveal the bird's location to predators. Birds also use mobbing calls to summon other birds, as chickadees and crows do when scolding and harassing owls and other unwanted visitors. Birds flying in flocks, like cedar waxwings, often call continuously. Such calls help birds migrating by night to stay together.

The study of bird dialects and experiments with birds that have been deafened or raised in isolation indicate that songs are genetically inherited only to a very crude extent. Although a few species, such as doves, sing well even when raised in isolation, most birds raised alone produce inferior, simplified songs. Generally, young songbirds learn their songs by listening to adult birds and by practice singing, called *subsong*. Yet birds raised in isolation and exposed to many tape-recorded songs show an innate preference for the songs of their own species.

Probably the easiest way to learn bird songs is to listen repeatedly to recordings and to refer at the same time to a standard field guide. Most guides describe bird vocalizations with such terms as *harsh, nasal, flutelike, piercing, plaintive, wavering, twittering, buzzing, sneezy,* and *sputtering.* Played slowly, bird recordings demonstrate that the songs contain many more notes than the human ear ordinarily hears.

Shape is one of the first and most important aspects to notice once you actually see a bird. Most birds can at least be placed in the proper family and many species can be identified by shape or silhouette, without reference to other field marks. Some birds, such as kestrels, are distinctly stocky, big-headed, and powerful-looking, while others, such as catbirds and cuckoos, are elegantly long and slender. Kingfishers, blue jays, tufted titmice, Bohemian and cedar waxwings, and cardinals are among the few birds with crests.

Bird bills frequently have distinctive shapes and, more than any other body part, show adaptation to food supply. The beak can be chunky, like that of a grosbeak, to crack seeds; thin and curved, like that of a creeper, to probe bark for insects; hooked, like that of a shrike, to tear at flesh; long and slender, like that of a hummingbird, to sip nectar from tubular flowers; or some other characteristic shape depending on the bird's food. Goatsuckers, swifts, flycatchers, and swallows, all of which catch flying insects, have widely hinged bills and gaping mouths. The long, thin bills of starlings and meadowlarks are suited to probing the ground. In the Galapagos Islands west of Ecuador, Charles Darwin noted fourteen species of finches, each of which had evolved a different type of beak or style of feeding that gave it a competitive advantage for a particular type of food. Many birds are nonetheless flexible about their diet, especially from season to season when food sources change or become scarce. For example, Tennessee warblers, which ordinarily glean insects from foliage, also take large amounts of nectar from tropical flowers when wintering in South and Central America.

In addition to beaks, nearly every other part of a bird's body is adapted to help exploit its environment. Feet of passerines, or songbirds, are adapted to perching, with three toes in front and one long toe behind; waterfowl have webbed or lobed feet for swimming; and raptors have talons for grasping prey.

Other key elements of body shape are the length and form of wings, tails, and legs. The wings may be long, pointed, and developed for swift, sustained flight, like those of falcons. Or the wings may be short and rounded for abrupt bursts of speed, like those of accipiters. The tail may have a deep fork like that of a barn swallow, a shallow notch like that of a tree swallow, a square tip like that of a cliff swallow, or a round tip like that of a blue jay.

Size is difficult to estimate and therefore not very useful in identifying birds. The best approach is to bear in mind the relative sizes of different species and to use certain well-known birds like the chickadee, sparrow, robin, kingfisher, and crow as standards for mental comparison. For example, if a bird resembles a song sparrow but looks unusually large, it might be a fox sparrow.

Plumage, whether plain or princely, muted or magnificent, is one of the most obvious keys to identification. Color can occur in remarkable combinations of spots, stripes, streaks, patches, and other patterns that make even supposedly drab birds a pleasure to see. In some instances, like the brown streaks of American bitterns and many other species, the plumage provides camouflage. Most vireos and warblers are various shades and combinations of yellow, green, brown, gray, and black, as one would expect from their forest environment. The black and white backs of woodpeckers help them to blend in with bark dappled with sunlight. The bold patterns of killdeers and some other plovers break up their outlines in much the same manner that warships used to be camouflaged before the invention of radar. Many shore birds display countershading: they are dark above and light below, a pattern that reduces the effect of shadows and makes them appear an inconspicuous monotone. Even some brightly colored birds have camouflaging plumages when they are young and least able to avoid predators.

For some species, it is important not to be camouflaged. Many sea birds are mostly white, which in all light conditions enables them to be seen at great distances against the water. Because flocks of sea birds spread out from their colonies to search for food, it is vital that a bird that has located food be visible to others after it has landed on the water to feed.

To organize the immense variation of plumages, focus on different basic elements and ask the following types of questions. Starting with the head, is it uniformly colored like that of the red-headed woodpecker? Is there a small patch on the crown, like that of Wilson's warbler and the ruby-crowned kinglet, or a larger cap on the front and top of the head, like that of the common redpoll and American goldfinch? Is the crown striped like the ovenbird's? Does a ring surround the eye, as with a Connecticut warbler, or are the eye rings perhaps even joined across the top of the bill to form spectacles, like those of a yellow-breasted chat? Is there a stripe over or through the eyes, like the red-breasted nuthatch's, or a conspicuous black mask across the eyes, like that of a common yellowthroat or loggerhead shrike? From the head go on to the rest of the body, where distinctive colors and patterns can also mark a bird's bill, throat, breast, belly, back, sides, wings, rump, tail, and legs.

Finally, what a bird *does* is an important clue to its identity. Certain habits, postures, ways of searching for food, and other behavior characterize different species. Some passerines, such as larks, juncos, and towhees, are strictly ground feeders; other birds, including flycatchers and swallows, nab insects on the wing; and others, such as nuthatches and creepers, glean insects from the crevices in bark. Woodpeckers bore into the bark. Vireos and most warblers pick insects from the foliage of trees and brush.

All of these birds may be further distinguished by other habits of eating. For example, towhees scratch for insects and
seeds by kicking backward with both feet together, whereas
juncos rarely do, although both hop to move along the ground.
Other ground feeders, such as meadowlarks, walk rather than
hop. Despite the children's song, robins generally run, not
hop. Swallows catch insects while swooping and skimming in
continuous flight, but flycatchers dart out from a limb, grab an
insect (sometimes with an audible smack), and then return to
their perch. Brown creepers have the curious habit of system-
atically searching for food by climbing trees in spirals, then
flying back to the ground to climb again. Woodpeckers tend to
hop upward, bracing themselves against the tree with their stiff
tails. Nuthatches walk up and down trees and branches head
first, seemingly without regard for gravity. Vireos are sluggish
compared to the hyperactive, flitting warblers.

Many birds divide a food source into zones, an arrangement
that apparently evolved to ensure each species its own food
supply. The short-legged green heron sits at the edge of the
water or on a low overhanging branch, waiting for its prey to
come close to shore. Medium-sized black-crowned and
yellow-crowned night herons hunt in shallow water. The long-
legged great blue heron stalks fish in water up to two feet deep.
Swans, geese, and many ducks graze underwater on the stems
and tubers of grassy plants, but the longer necks of swans and
geese enable them to reach deeper plants. Similarly, different
species of shore birds take food from the same mud flat by
probing with their varied bills to different depths. Species of
warblers that feed in the same tree are reported to concentrate
in separate areas among the trunk, twig tips, tree top, and
ground. Starlings and cowbirds feeding in flocks on the ground
show another arrangement that provides an even distribution of
food: those in the rear fly ahead to the front, so that the entire
flock rolls slowly across the field.

Different species also have different styles of flight. Soaring
is typical of some big birds. Gulls float nearly motionless in
the wind. Buteos and turkey vultures soar on updrafts in wide

circles, although turkey vultures may be further distinguished by wings held in a shallow V. Some other large birds, such as accipiters, rarely soar but instead interrupt their wing beats with glides. Kestrels, terns, and kingfishers can hover in one spot. Hummingbirds, like oversized dragonflies, can also hover and even fly backward. Slightly more erratic than the swooping, effortless flight of swallows is that of swifts, flitting with wing beats that appear to alternate (but do not). Still other birds, such as the American goldfinch and flickers, dip up and down in wavelike flight. Some species, including jays and grackles, fly dead straight. Among ducks, the surface-feeding species launch themselves directly upward into flight, seeming to jump from the water, but the heavy diving ducks typically patter along the surface before becoming airborne.

Various idiosyncracies distinguish yet other species. The spotted sandpiper and northern waterthrush walk with a teetering, bobbing motion. Coots pump their heads back and forth as they swim. The eastern phoebe regularly jerks its tail downward while perching, but wrens often cock their tails vertically. Herons and egrets fly with their necks folded back; storks, ibises, and cranes fly with their necks outstretched. Still other birds have characteristic postures while sitting or flying or other unique habits that provide a reliable basis for identification.

BUS: From downtown Baltimore, take MTA bus #27 via Howard Street, Remington Avenue, and Falls Road to Mt. Washington Village at the intersection of Falls Road and Kelly Avenue. You will know that your stop is coming after the bus crosses Northern Parkway.

From the intersection with Kelly Avenue, walk north 0.5 mile on Falls Road to the park entrance on the right immediately before the long bridge over Jones Falls. Follow the entrance road to the intersection with Hollins Avenue. Be alert for cars; where there is no sidewalk, walk on the road's left shoulder to minimize the risk of being hit by a car approaching from behind.

AUTOMOBILE: Robert E. Lee Park (perhaps better known simply as Lake Roland) is located just north of Baltimore. The entrance is on Falls Road a few blocks north of Mt. Washington Village.

From Interstate 83 (Jones Falls Expressway) inside the Beltway, take the exit for Northern Parkway. (If you are approaching from the south, there are two exits at Northern Parkway; take the eastbound exit.) Follow Northern Parkway east a few hundred yards to an intersection with Falls Road, and there turn left. Follow Falls Road 0.9 mile. Just before the long bridge over Jones Falls, turn right onto the entrance road to Robert E. Lee Memorial Park. Go 0.4 mile to an intersection with Hollins Avenue (which provides an alternative means of approach from Lake Avenue). Continue straight to the parking lot.

WALK: Cross the bridge just below the dam, then follow an asphalt path, at one point forking right along the water's edge. After circling along the shore, continue gradually uphill past a shelter at the top of the knoll. Just beyond the shelter, turn right onto a rough dirt path leading downhill and along the shore to a railroad. As noted below and shown on the map, the route crosses the railroad, which was rarely used as of 1987. However, it is possible that at some time in the future the line will be refurbished for use by commuter trains, perhaps even with an electrified third rail. Obviously, in this case you should not cross the tracks unless the park authorities have provided safe provision to do so (conceivably at some other location nearer the dam). It is not possible to predict what kind of warning signs, fences, or other safety measures will be provided if the railroad is refurbished, so be cautious. Incidentally, this railroad is the old Northern Central, of which the roadbed north of Cockeysville is now a hiker/biker trail, as described in Chapter 10.

With caution, cross the railroad and continue straight along the shore with the lake on your right. Where an earth ridge appears on the right, continue straight along a trough that gradually curves left. At a slightly skewed T-intersection, turn right for 30 yards, then bear left. Continue more or less straight through the woods to an old railroad bridge. Incidentally, the trail you have been following is the former roadbed of the Greenspring Valley Branch of the Northern Central Railroad.

With caution, cross the bridge, which is paved only with railroad ties. Immediately after crossing the bridge, turn right and descend steeply from the railroad embankment. With Jones Falls on your right, follow the path (sometimes obscure) through the streamside jungle. Continue as the path passes below houses on the left. Eventually, the trail reaches a road. Bear right on the road 40 yards, then turn right to follow the road across a bridge; be alert for cars. About 50 yards beyond the bridge, turn right at a gate. Follow a grassy track several hundred yards to a large meadow and playing field overlooking the marsh at the northern end of Lake Roland.

Return to the dam at the southern end of Lake Roland the way you came.

12

LOCH RAVEN

Southeast Narrows and Southern Shore

Walking—up to 10.0 miles (16.1 kilometers) round-trip. This long walk starts by following the shore of the reservoir along a portion of Loch Raven Road that is closed to cars on Saturday and Sunday between 10 AM and 5 PM. With its sweeping views over the water, the roadway provides a pleasant walk totaling 3.5 miles round-trip. For the full hike outlined on the map, continue on a dirt road that winds around wooded hillsides and ravines. The trail eventually ends by the water's edge at the tip of a peninsula. Return the way you came. If you are looking for a country setting in which to push your child in a stroller, Loch Raven Road makes an excellent promenade during the period it is closed to automobiles. Dogs must be leashed. Mangaged by Baltimore City Bureau of Water and Waste Water (telephone 795–6151).

LOCH RAVEN IS ONE of Baltimore City's three major reservoirs. The others are Prettyboy Reservoir, located upstream from Loch Raven on Big Gunpowder Falls, and Liberty Reservoir on the North Branch of the Patapsco River. Both Loch Raven and Liberty are terminal reservoirs—the last impoundments on their rivers before the water is removed and treated for drinking. Prettyboy Reservoir simply provides additional storage within the Gunpowder watershed. When the level of Loch Raven drops more than three feet below the crest of the dam, water is released from Prettyboy in order to maintain high

water in Loch Raven. As a result, the level of Prettyboy Reservoir fluctuates widely, as does the water in Big Gunpowder Falls above and below Loch Raven, depending on whether the reservoirs are being filled or spilled. Baltimore also has the right to pump water from the Philadelphia Electric Company's Conowingo Dam on the Susquehanna River, but it does so only in droughts or other emergencies.

To protect its water supply, Baltimore City owns about nine square miles of forested land surrounding each of its three reservoirs. In managing these buffer areas, the city has adopted a multiple-use policy that includes the harvesting of timber for municipal projects and allows a wide variety of recreational uses.

Timber cutting began on Baltimore's watershed properties in 1948, when the city decided to use the trees standing in the area that was to be flooded by the new Liberty Dam. The city hired a woods crew and purchased logging equipment and a saw mill. Selective cutting of hardwood trees has continued ever since to supply the Department of Public Works and other city departments with both crude and finished lumber, including shoring for trenches, fence posts, guardrails, pier timbers, and survey stakes. The city also harvests and sells pulpwood thinned from its watershed pine plantations. In 1986 the value of the lumber and pulpwood cut from the city's watersheds was $267,000.

The city's timber program is designed to avoid erosion and to minimize the unsightliness commonly associated with logging. Clear-cutting is done only in small areas; other, larger areas may be thinned. The forest on only about one-half of 1 percent of the city's watershed land is harvested each year. In areas that are heavily used by the public, logging is limited to salvaging dead or damaged trees. Yet despite these and other precautions, the city often receives complaints from dismayed preservationists urging that the forests should not be touched.

Although Baltimore's watershed properties are not public parks, the city also tries, as a part of its multiple-use policy, to accommodate recreational activities that are compatible with

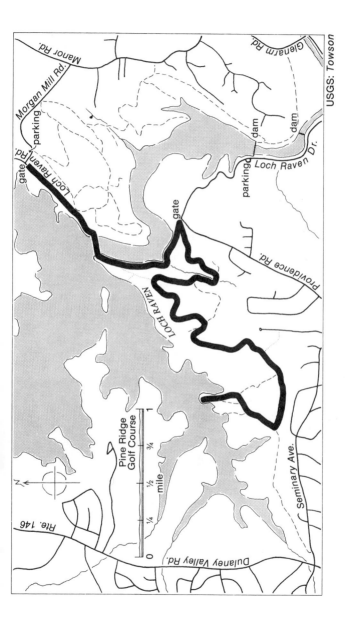

USGS: Towson

Manor Rd.

Morgan Mill Rd.

parking

gate

gate

Loch Raven Rd.

Glenarm Rd.

dam

dam

Loch Raven Dr.

parking

gate

Providence Rd.

LOCH RAVEN

Pine Ridge
Golf Course

N

0   ¼   ½   ¾   1

mile

Rte. 146

Dulaney Valley Rd.

Seminary Ave.

the higher priorities of water protection and forest management. Permitted activities include fishing, hiking, and horseback riding. Eighteen hundred boat permits are distributed annually, but no gasoline motors or sailboats are allowed. Rowboats can be rented at the Loch Raven Fishing Center off Dulaney Valley Road. An eighteen-hole municipal golf course has long existed at Pine Ridge on the shore of Loch Raven, and another adjacent course is planned.

The controversy that has erupted over this proposed new golf course epitomizes the problems of balancing water quality and recreation. There is little doubt that a second golf course, if built, would be very popular and heavily patronized. But opponents point out that golf courses are notorious users of lawn chemicals, and that the new course would increase the flow of fertilizers and weed killers into the reservoir, which already has an intractable problem with algal blooms from excessive nutrients.

As of mid-1987, Baltimore City's Board of Estimates had tentatively approved the new golf course, but had also established an environmental management committee to study prospective problems and to specify various safeguards that will have to be implemented before construction of a second golf course can go ahead. The contemplated safeguards include a 50-foot buffer of undisturbed vegetation along the shore of Loch Raven, devices to encourage infiltration of rain rather than surface runoff, and listing and logging of chemicals spread on the golf course.

These measures have been recommended by the city's watershed managers, who nonetheless question their efficacy and would prefer that the new golf course not be built at all. William Wolinski, the city's water quality coordinator for the Department of Public Works, has pointed out that the city owns only 6 percent of the Big Gunpowder watershed and should anticipate continuing deterioration of environmental conditions on the remaining 94 percent over which it has little or no control. Under these circumstances, many people question whether it makes sense to downgrade the city's limited watershed land—its last line of defense against pollution—by converting between 60 and 80 acres to a new golf course that will itself be a source of pollution.

Whatever the outcome of the golf course controversy (a matter in which you may want to play a role by writing to the mayor), the range of recreation allowed on Baltimore's watershed lands is very liberal compared to activities permitted on other municipal reservoirs in the East. According to a survey conducted in 1968 by the United States Forest Service's Northeastern Forest Experiment Station, boating was allowed at only 11 percent of municipal reservoirs in the Northeast and Mid-Atlantic regions, fishing at 39 percent, picnicking at 19 percent, hiking at 35 percent, horseback riding at 14 percent, and hunting at 40 percent. Camping and swimming, both prohibited at Baltimore's reservoirs, were permitted respectively at 9 percent and 4 percent of reservoirs. Baltimore's watershed managers, however, point out that opportunities for camping and swimming are already available at state and county parks near Baltimore.

Whether boating on reservoirs or hiking, riding, or picnicking in their surrounding watersheds significantly impairs water quality is unknown. What little research has been done has produced inconclusive results. But other management problems caused by large numbers of visitors are only too clear. Baltimore, for example, has closed its picnic area at Loch Raven and has curtailed use of the Liberty Dam overlook because crowds and drinking were getting out of hand. Also, litter is pervasive, thrown overboard from boats, scattered at fishing spots along the shore, and heaped at focal points such as the trailhead below Prettyboy Dam. Another bane is motorized trailbikes. Even horseback riding has become a nuisance in some places as dirt roads have been kneaded into quagmires and gullies. In the Forest Service survey noted earlier, over a third of the managers of watersheds where recreation was permitted indicated that recreation caused serious problems.

Recreational use of reservoirs and watersheds also increases administrative burdens. Areas popular with visitors have to be patrolled more often to enforce watershed regulations. (Incidentally, watershed police have full power to issue citations and to arrest offenders.) Although much of the responsibility for overseeing the wide range of programs at Baltimore's reservoirs has fallen on the city's Watershed Section, some of the administrative duties have been given to other agencies with a more immediate interest in public recreation. The Baltimore Municipal Golf Corporation operates Pine Ridge Golf Course at Loch Raven, and the Baltimore County Department of Recreation and Parks runs the Loch Raven boat rental and fishing concession (252–8755). Similarly, state Fish and Wildlife Administration officers assist in enforcing the city's ban on firearms.

In summary, the residents of the Baltimre region are very fortunate that the area's reservoirs and watershed lands are open to public use. The continuation of this policy, however, depends on the cooperation and reasonable behavior of those who use these areas.

AUTOMOBILE: Loch Raven is located north of Baltimore. The walk described here starts on Loch Raven Road at the intersection with Morgan Mill Road.

From Interstate 695 (the Beltway) north of Baltimore, take exit 27 for Route 146 north. Follow Route 146 north about 4.2 miles. Immediately after crossing a bridge over Loch Raven, bear right on Dulaney Valley Road where Jarrettsville Pike heads left. Follow Dulaney Valley Road 1.7 miles. Where Dulaney Valley Road turns left at Peerce's Plantation Restaurant, continue straight on Loch Raven Road. Go 1.0 mile to the intersection of Loch Raven Road and Morgan Mill Road. South of this intersection, Loch Raven Road is closed to automobile traffic between 10 AM and 5 PM on Saturday and Sunday. Park near the intersection; pay close attention to signs indicating where parking is permitted and where it is not.

WALK: From the intersection of Loch Raven Road and Morgan Mill Road, pass the orange gate and follow Loch Raven Road, with the reservoir on your right. Follow the road along the edge of the reservoir, across a bridge, and gradually uphill to another orange gate at the intersection of Providence Road and Loch Raven Drive.

Immediately beyond the orange gate, turn right past a green gate and enter the woods on a fire road. Follow the fire road through the woods, then through a clearing and back into the woods. Continue on the main track past obscure side trails. Eventually, the path climbs obliquely along the side of a large ravine. Part way up the hill, fork right. Continue obliquely uphill, with the slope falling off to your right. Follow the trail along the contour of the hill. Stay on the main track. During the leafless seasons, Loch Raven is visible to the right.

Continue as the trail winds, dips, and climbs along the hillside. Eventually, at a major intersection, bear right downhill (where the other trail climbs left). Go 150 yards. At a fork in the trail, bear left along the hillside and around the shoulder of the hill to the left. Continue on the main track as the trail winds, climbs, and dips along the hillside for about a mile. Again, ignore obscure side trails.

Continue as the terrain become less hilly and the woods less mature—that is, as the trees get smaller and the understory becomes choked with vines and scrubby growth. Eventually, after passing a long series of houses visible one after another through the woods to the left, turn right at a major intersection.

Continue through the woods. At a fork in the trail, bear right. Go 230 yards, then fork right again where an obscure trail veers left. After 70 yards, bear left where a trail intersects from the right. Continue straight to the water's edge near the tip of a promontory.

Return to the starting point the way you came.

13

LOCH RAVEN

Southeast Highlands

Walking and ski touring—3.0 miles (4.8 kilometers). Follow a circuit of fire roads through the woods overlooking Loch Raven. A spur trail leads through a deep ravine to a remote promontory north of the dam. The watershed land is open daily from sunrise to sunset. Dogs must be leashed. Managed by the Baltimore City Bureau of Water and Waste Water (telephone 795–6151).

ALTHOUGH BALTIMORE CITY owns about nine square miles of watershed land surrounding each of its three reservoirs, its property amounts to less than 6 percent of the 303 square miles in the Big Gunpowder Falls drainage area above Loch Raven Dam and also less than 6 percent of the 164 square miles in the Patapsco watershed above Liberty Dam. No part of these two drainage areas is within the city. The resulting lack of control over the watershed greatly complicates protection of Baltimore's water supply, which also serves much of the metropolitan region.

Sedimentation, for example, is a major problem largely traceable to erosion on land that is not controlled by the city. According to a study of the Baltimore region conducted in 1977 by the Soil Conservation Service, annually cultivated cropland contributed about half of the nearly one million tons of sediment—the equivalent of 20,000 freight cars full—that were estimated to wash into the waters of the Baltimore area

yearly. Yet various conservation measures—such as contour plowing, strip cropping, terracing, gully control, and no-till planting—that in 1977 were used on only 32 percent of the farmland in the Baltimre region, reduced soil loss on that land by 80 percent. Even if only very approximate, these figures at least give some idea of the magnitude of Baltimore's interest in what happens on the surrounding farmland, since much of the sediment ends up in the city's reservoirs, as indicated by periodic depth surveys. Erosion from farmland not only clogs streams and reduces the storage capacity of the reservoirs, but also increases turbidity and pollution from fertilizers, animal wastes, and pesticides with which the mud is permeated.

Another major source of sediments is large-scale residential and commercial development entailing the stripping and grading of huge tracts of land. Again, according to the 1977 report of the Soil Conservation Service, the amount of soil loss per acre on land undergoing development is about fifteen times greater than on land in cultivated row crops, forty-four times greater than land in pasture, and sixty-three times greater than on land in timber. Thus, even though only a small percentage of land is undergoing development at any time, erosion from construction sites contributes disproportionately to stream sedimentation.

To reduce erosion and sedimentation, Maryland adopted a Sediment Control Law in 1970 requiring that all construction projects be carried out in accordance with a grading and sediment control plan approved by the local Soil Conservation District. City and county development permit agencies are supposed to inspect construction sites and to enforce the required sediment control measures, such as dikes to divert stormwater runoff around the sites, straw mulch to cushion the impact of rain and to slow runoff, and basins to allow sediments to settle before the water flows from the sites. At first, enforcement of such measures was lax, but government agencies and development contractors have been more observant of the law in recent years.

The dependence of Baltimore City on the cooperation of

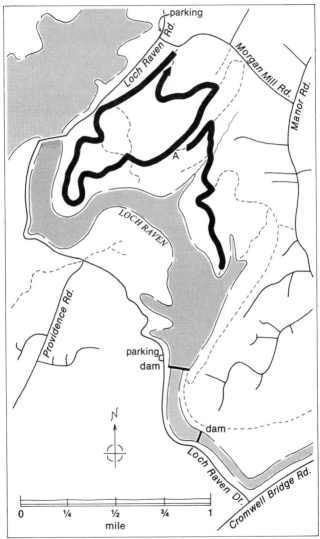

parking

Loch Raven Rd.

Morgan Mill Rd.

Manor Rd.

A

LOCH RAVEN

Providence Rd.

parking
dam

dam

Loch Raven Dr.

Cromwell Bridge Rd.

N

0   ¼   ½   ¾   1
mile

USGS: *Towson*

county Soil Conservation Districts and development permit agencies to encourage soil conservation practices and to enforce sediment control laws is typical of the economic and environmental dilemma faced by Baltimore's watershed managers. Several jurisdictions are involved, and often a cheap solution for one area's wastewater problem imposes injury and expense on another. For example, in 1972 tests conducted by the federal Environmental Protection Agency indicated that algae growth in Loch Raven was rampant, stimulated in part by phosphates in the effluent from the Manchester and Hampstead sewage treatment plants in Carroll County. Equipment to remove some of the phosphorus was not installed until five years later, after Baltimore City, Baltimore County, Carroll County, and the state contributed the necessary funds.

A comprehensive and coordinated program to combat water pollution is the object of an agreement reached in 1984 among Baltimore City, Baltimore and Carroll counties, and the state. The program of action that has grown out of this agreement stresses several approaches to reduce chemical pollution and sedimentation. At the state level, the Department of the Environment is supposed to use its system of discharge permits to tighten control over municipal and industrial effluents from so-called point sources of pollution—that is, pollution that comes from specific major sources, such as food processing plants. The sewage treatment plant at Hampstead will be upgraded still further (as has been done several times already), and at Manchester sewage effluent will be sprayed onto land instead of dumped into Big Gunpowder Falls.

As significant as pollution from point sources is, on a cumulative basis it is thought to be equaled or exceeded by pollution from nonpoint sources—that is, myriad sources such as stormwater runoff from fertilized fields, dairy pastures, livestock feedlots, and urban streets. Because of its widespread nature, nonpoint pollution is a particularly intractable problem.

Regarding agricultural pollution, the Soil Conservation Districts of Baltimore and Carroll counties are supposed to take the lead toward reducing erosion from farm fields and effluents from livestock wastes. The cooperation of farmers is sought with a carrot-and-stick approach. The carrot is the lure of assistance from state and federal agriculture departments to implement better farming practices, and the stick is the threat of legal action by the state Department of the Environment.

In more developed areas, the county health departments are charged with the responsibility to correct sanitation problems found in many old subdivisions and once-rural communities—problems such as failing septic systems, overburdened sewers, and pumping stations that regularly leak or overflow into local streams.

In Baltimore County and to a lesser extent in Carroll County, policies have also been adopted to steer development away from sensitive areas, such as stream banks, flood plains, wetlands, and steep slopes. These policies are implemented by a process for reviewing construction projects on a case-by-case basis, and also by zoning. For example, in 1976 Baltimore County established a new Watershed Protection Zone covering areas near reservoirs and large tributaries. As of 1987 the minimum lot size in the Watershed Protection Zone was three acres.

As areas become more urbanized, stormwater runoff from streets and parking lots becomes a major source of pollution. Not only is surface runoff from such areas contaminated with oil residues, toxic metals, and other wastes, but also the sheer volume of runoff is increased by the development of land. Experiments conducted at Liberty Reservoir indicate that when land is cleared of trees and planted in grass, annual runoff increases up to 30 percent because less water is returned to the atmosphere through transpiration and evaporation from leaf and bark surfaces. Similarly, large impervious surfaces intercept water that to some extent would have soaked into the ground. Instead, storm sewers quickly flush the water into streams, loading the rivers with filth, swelling peak volumes, and increasing erosive energy. To prevent this surge of stormwater runoff, some environmentalists are urging that subdivision requirements for extensive storm sewers, gutters, and curbs be relaxed, and that greater use be made instead of permeable riprap drainage swales and infiltration basins to slow stormwater runoff, filter out dirt and debris, and increase percolation into the ground.

AUTOMOBILE: Loch Raven is located north of Baltimore. The walk described here starts near the intersection of Loch Raven Road and Morgan Mill Road.

From Interstate 695 (the Beltway) north of Baltimore, take exit 27 for Route 146 north. Follow Route 146 north about 4.2 miles. Immediately after crossing a bridge over Loch Raven, bear right on Dulaney Valley Road where Jarrettsville Pike heads left. Follow Dulaney Valley Road 1.7 miles. Where Dulaney Valley Road turns left at Peerce's Plantation Restaurant, continue straight on Loch Raven Road. Go 1.0 mile to the intersection of Loch Raven Road and Morgan Mill Road. Park near the intersection; pay close attention to signs indicating where parking is permitted and where (or when) it is not.

WALK: Start your walk on a fire road that leaves Morgan Mill Road 160 yards uphill from the intersection of Morgan Mill Road and Loch Raven Road. With the reservoir downhill to your right, enter the woods on the fire road and follow it along the hillside, passing (after only 90 yards) a trail intersecting from the left—and by which you will return at the end of the walk. Continue along the hillside, with the reservoir visible downhill to the right through the trees. Follow the trail as it gradually descends and passes a trail intersecting from the rear-left. Continue straight on the dirt trail as it passes a dozen yards above Loch Raven Road, then curves left uphill along the side of a small ravine. Follow the trail up the ravine for about 200 yards, then turn right at the first trail junction. Follow a wide path up and over a hill and then around to the left, with the land sloping off to the right toward the reservoir.

Follow the path as it eventually climbs to a four-way

trail junction, and there turn right. After only 50 yards, pass a trail intersecting from the right. Continue straight gradually uphill, then along a plateau. At an intersection marked A on the map, pass a trail leading downhill to the right (unless you want to follow the spur trail to the iso- lated promontory north of the dam, as shown on the map, and as is well worthwhile).

From point A on the map, continue along the plateau. Turn left at the next trail junction and follow the path through the woods, then gradually downhill and to the right. Pass obscure side trails as the main path descends obliquely along the side of the hill, with the slope falling off to your left. Continue downhill to a trail junction within sight of your starting point at Morgan Mill Road.

14

GUNPOWDER FALLS STATE PARK

Belair Road to Harford Road

Walking and ski touring—up to 9.0 miles (14.5 kilometers) round-trip. Follow a footpath along the river bank through a deep, wooded valley. Continue as far as you want, then return the way you came. The trail is rough but easily passable. Although close to the city and the surrounding suburbia, this gorge is a remarkable wilderness enclave. The park is open daily from sunrise to sunset. Dogs must be leashed. Managed by the Maryland Park Service (telephone 592–2897).

THIS WALK is the first of three starting at the Belair Road bridge and focusing on the stretch of Big Gunpowder Falls below Loch Raven dam. Upstream on the south bank, the riverside path extends to the Harford Road bridge through one of the deepest parts of the Big Gunpowder gorge. On the north bank upstream from Belair Road, the circle path explores the valley slopes and upland. Downstream, the trail follows the river toward the edge of the fall line zone where the Gunpowder leaves its Piedmont valley and enters the Coastal Plain. Throughout the length of all three excursions, the valley slopes are covered with deep woods. At high water the river is swift, powerful, and sometimes turbulent. At low water (or no water), its bed is a broad, bare swath of cobbles and boulders.

If by now you have taken some of the walks outlined in this book, you have probably noticed a certain sameness in our local landscape. With the exception of Anne Arundel County, the

countryside in the Baltimore region is characterized by rolling uplands dissected by an intricate system of ravines, valleys, and gorges. This landscape provides as good an example as any of the erosional cycle by which running water carves into an elevated region and over the ages reduces it to a lower plain.

Stream erosion is the dominant force shaping the world's landforms. Whenever any part of the earth's crust is raised above sea level, either by uplift of the land or withdrawal of the ocean as water is amassed in continental glaciers, the newly elevated surface is at once subject to the erosive power of running water. Any downward-pitched trough, crevice, or fissure, even though at first shallow or insignificant, is self-aggrandizing, collecting the rainwater that falls on other areas. Initially, such minor watercourses are dry between rains, but gradually they deepen with erosion, and once they penetrate the water table, they are fed by a steady seepage of groundwater from the sides of the gullies and ravines.

As a stream extends itself by developing tributaries, its erosive power rapidly increases. The larger drainage area concentrates more water in the channel downstream, where stream energy is swelled both by the greater mass of moving water and by its greater depth, which results in proportionately less friction with the stream bed. In consequence, the speed of the river increases and so does its ability to carry fine clay, silt, and sand in suspension and to push and roll pebbles and cobbles downstream.

Although at first erosion is fastest in the lower reaches of a river where volume is greater, ponds, lakes, and ultimately the ocean constitute a base level below which the stream cannot cut to any significant degree. As downward cutting approaches the base level, the site of the most rapid erosion moves slowly upstream.

Meanwhile, the lower river still possesses great energy. The current erodes the bank wherever the stream is deflected by each slight turn. This tendency to carve wider and wider curves is present along the entire stream but is accentuated in the

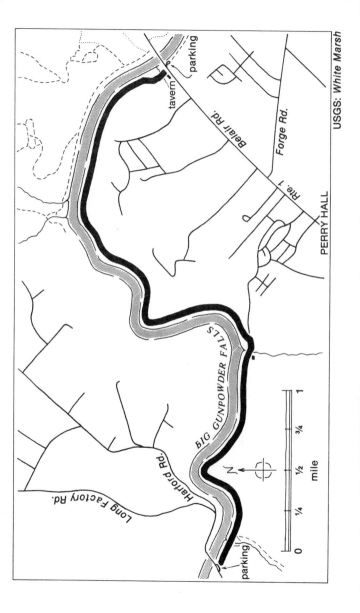

USGS: White Marsh

lower reaches, where downward cutting is no longer possible but where sideward cutting can continue as long as there is flow. Gradually, a meandering course develops as the river snakes back and forth, eroding first one side of the valley and then the other. When sinuosity becomes so extreme that the river doubles back on itself, the current will intercept the channel farther downstream, cutting off the looping meader. Thus, as millenia pass, the river migrates in an everchanging course over the bottomland, creating a valley much wider than it is deep and leaving behind abandoned channels here and there.

Another distinctive geologic feature develops at the mouth of the river where it empties into an ocean, estuary, or lake. As the current dissipates in the standing water, the capacity of the stream to carry material in suspension is reduced and then eliminated, so that the river's load of gravel, sand, and silt is dropped and forms a delta, as has occurred where Big Gunpowder Falls flows into Chesapeake Bay. Because the current slows gradually, the deposits tend to be sorted, with larger, heavier particles dropped first (all very convenient for the sand and gravel companies that mine these areas). After the delta has extended itself a considerable distance in one direction, a flood may cut a new and shorter channel to open water, causing the former course to be abandoned, at least for a period. Deltas typically have several channels or sets of channels between which the stream shifts as deposits are concentrated first in one and then in another.

Examining the variables of stream gradient, valley depth, valley width, and number of meanders will indicate the stage of development that has been reached by any stretch of river. In the earliest stage, gullies and ravines eat into the elevated land surface. Because the dominant direction of cutting is downward, the gullies and ravines are steep-sided and V-shaped, eventually becoming major valleys. The gradient of the steambed is steep compared to navigable waterways. Rapids are common. There are no flats in the valley bottom. Valley depth relative to width is at its maximum. Such a stream is said to be in *youth*.

As the stream approaches base level, its gradient diminishes and downward cutting slows. Bends in the course of the stream become accentuated, and the width of the valley increases relative to its depth. At the point where sideward cutting becomes significant and a flat valley floor starts to develop, the stream is said to be in *maturity.*

Finally, when downward cutting has ceased and the stream is at base level, sideward cutting produces a nearly flat and featureless valley, much wider than it is deep, across which the river meanders from side to side. Such an eroded surface is called a *peneplain.* The gradient is low and the broad bottomland is marked only by the scars, swamps, and lakes left by former channels. Perhaps a few rock hummocks and hills—more resistant to erosion than were their surroundings—are left rising above the plain. This stage of river development is *old age.* Meanwhile, the countless gullies and ravines at the river's headwaters remain youthful as they continue to fan outward like the roots of a growing tree, so that the watershed becomes larger and larger, perhaps even intercepting and diverting to itself streams that previously took a different course to the sea.

The terms *youth, maturity,* and *old age* can also be applied to an entire landscape or region to describe the extent to which it has been acted upon by stream erosion. As an upland region experiences the headward erosion of a stream system, more and more of the landscape is given over to a branching network of steep-sided gullies, ravines, and valleys, which gradually widen and develop flat valley bottoms. An area is said to be in youth until about half of the original upland is consumed by valley slopes and the streams are just beginning to develop flats at the valley bottoms. As the percentage of upland diminishes and the portion in the valley flats increases, the area is in maturity. At some point the upland lying between different stream systems is cut away until the divide changes from a wide, flat summit to a sharp-crested ridge that in turn is worn down to a low, rounded rise. Old age is said to start when more than half of the region is in valley bottom, and it continues as the whole region is gradually reduced to a peneplain. Thus, in general, youth is the time of dominant upland, maturity the time of dominant valley slope, and old age the time of dominant valley bottom.

Such, at any rate, is the general model. Of course, the terms *youth, maturity,* and *old age* do not describe the actual age of a stream or landscape, but only its stage of erosional development. Also, the appearance of any particular stretch of river is determined largely by the durability and structure of the materials through which the stream flows, and the terrain along even a single river can reflect different stages of erosion in no particular sequence, depending on the underlying materials.

Turning to the Maryland landscape at hand, as you approach Big Gunpowder Falls and walk along the river or through any of the other stream valleys discussed in this book, study the landscape to determine the degree to which it conforms to the pattern outlined here.

AUTOMOBILE: The section of Gunpowder Falls State Park explored by this walk is located northeast of Baltimore. The walk starts where Belair Road crosses Big Gunpowder Falls.

From Interstate 695 (the Beltway) northeast of Baltimore, take exit 32B for Route 1 north toward Bel Air. Follow Route 1 (Belair Road) about 5.3 miles to the bridge over Big Gunpowder Falls. A very small, obscure gravel parking area is located on the right side of the road just before the bridge, so be prepared to slow down and pull off the road.

WALK: From the parking area described above, cross Belair Road; there is no traffic light, so be cautious.

With the river toward your right and starting 35 yards away from the south end of the Belair Road bridge, follow a gravel drive briefly downhill next to a tavern. Continue straight across a grassy area. Cross a stream and continue straight on a narrow footpath that winds through the woods and eventually reaches the river's edge. For the first 0.25 mile, the trail is in poor condition and is obstructed by log and rock hurdles erected by local residents to discourage trailbikers. Conditions improve once the trail reaches the river.

With the water on your right, follow the riverside footpath for as long as you care to walk, keeping in mind that you will return by the same route. Be alert for places where the trail is undermined by erosion. The path stretches 4.5 miles to Harford Road. At 3.0 miles, the trail passes to the right of a brick structure and electric substation, then continues along the river's edge. Near Harford Road the trail fords a stream, which during high water, can be more easily crossed on the rocks a few dozen yards upstream; do not cross, however, if the water is flowing over the rocks.

The headquarters for Gunpowder Falls State Park is on the north bank of the river a short distance below the Harford Road bridge. Along this section of Harford Road are also several stone structures (some of them have been converted to private residences) that were originally part of the Gunpowder Copper Works. The copper works were constructed some time after 1811 by Levi Hollingsworth, who supplied the United States Navy with copper sheathing for ships during the War of 1812. His plant also rolled the copper for the dome of the national Capitol when it was rebuilt after the original building had been burned by the British in 1814. Hollingsworth's dome lasted until the 1860s. The copper works remained in operation until some time in the 1860s or '70s.

15

GUNPOWDER FALLS STATE PARK

Stockdale Road and Valley Rim

Walking and ski touring—3.5 miles (5.6 kilometers). From Belair Road head upstream along the river's edge on old Stockdale Road, a gravel and dirt path closed to cars. The path eventually climbs the side of the valley. Return on dirt roads and footpaths through former farmland now planted in pines. The park is open daily from sunrise to sunset. Dogs must be leashed. Managed by the Maryland Park Service (telephone 592–2897).

I**N TERMS OF THE STAGES** of stream development discussed in the preceding chapter, the stretch of Big Gunpowder Falls traversed by this walk is still young. The river flows in a steep-sided valley. Narrow strips of bottomland flats occur only at intervals along the banks. Although the gorge itself twists and turns, the channel does not meander but rather is confined by the valley walls.

However, three miles below the Belair Road bridge the river leaves its rocky Piedmont valley and flows out over the Coastal Plain, composed of gravel, sand, and clay deposited either as marine or delta sediments during periods when the region was submerged beneath the ocean. As would be expected, the relative ease of erosion in the soft sediments has enabled the rivers that cross the coastal zone to advance rapidly into maturity and even old age. For example, when Big Gunpowder Falls reaches the Coastal Plain, the valley walls dwindle and disappear. The

river flows slowly within mud and gravel banks over a broad lowland marked by former channels that are now located far from the present course of the river. The Gunpowder has even had time to develop a large delta in the vicinity of Days Cove.

Marking the transition between Piedmont and Coastal Plain is the so-called fall line, which is not really a sharp line but rather a zone of considerable width. Within the fall line zone the uplands are covered by a tapering layer of Coastal Plain sediments, but the stream channels penetrate into the underlying Piedmont rocks. Also, waterfalls and rapids are not confined to the fall zone but frequently extend dozens of miles upstream, as is the case on the Gunpowder Falls and Patapsco River. In Maryland, the tracks of the Baltimore & Ohio Railroad follow the edge of the fall zone because the route combines level terrain with narrow river crossings.

Although in most respects Big Gunpowder Falls conforms to the pattern of stream development discussed in the preceding chapter, several anomalies exist. One curiosity is that some of the Gunpowder's tributary valleys, such as the Dulaney and Cockeysville valleys, have smooth, broad (in other words, old) profiles compared to the relatively youthful main gorge farther downstream, even though the tributaries necessarily are of more recent origin than the section of river below them. The tributaries, it turns out, flow through areas underlain by Cockeysville marble, which (because it is limestone) dissolves more easily than the gneiss, serpentine, granite, gabbro, and other hard crystalline rocks that predominate throughout the region. Thus, the terrain along a river can reflect different stages of erosional development in no particular sequence, depending on the underlying rock.

The variety of rock types, their different degrees of resistance to erosion, and the complications in their structural relations may also have contributed to some of the abrupt twists and turns that occur in the valley of Big Gunpowder Falls. For the most part, however, the Gunpowder and its many tributaries show the spreading, rootlike pattern of a dendritic stream

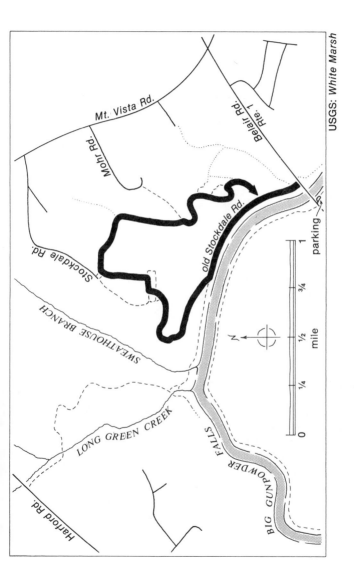

USGS: White Marsh

system, as is typical in areas where there is no systematic rock structure that guides the pattern of erosion.

Another anomaly is evident in Maryland's Piedmont upland, which consists of rolling hills characteristic of a mature stream system. Yet this landscape is further dissected by a youthful system of gorges and ravines. The cause appears to be that the entire Piedmont, after being shaped by erosion into a region of moderate, rounded ridges and broad valleys, was uplifted. The rise of the land increased stream gradients and renewed the ability of rivers to erode downward. As a result, youthful gorges were cut into the old surface, producing the present landscape in which the gentle slopes and broad bottomlands of the former valleys remain as elevated shoulders above the entrenched gorges. In the terminology of geologists, such a process of regional uplift and renewed erosion is called *rejuvenation.*

There is evidence in Maryland and along the East Coast that the uplift of the Piedmont has not progressed at a steady rate relative to sea level, which itself has fluctuated as water has been amassed as ice during successive periods of continental glaciation. After each uplift, the land along the coast was exposed to the horizontal cutting action of waves and meandering rivers. In consequence, on a regional scale the topography of both the Piedmont and the Coastal Plain roughly forms a flight of terracelike surfaces that parallel the coast and even extend upstream in the major river valleys.

AUTOMOBILE: The section of Gunpowder Falls State Park explored by this walk is located northeast of Baltimore. The walk starts where Belair Road crosses Big Gunpowder Falls.

From Interstate 695 (the Beltway) northeast of Baltimore, take exit 32B for Route 1 north toward Bel Air. Follow Route 1 (Belair Road) north about 5.3 miles to the bridge over Big Gunpowder Falls. A very small, obscure gravel parking area is located on the right side of the road just before the bridge, so be prepared to slow down and pull off the road.

WALK: From the parking area described above, cross the bridge over Big Gunpowder Falls, then cross Belair Road; there is no traffic light here, so be cautious.

Start your walk on the wide path entering the woods at the north end of the Belair Road bridge. With the river on your left, follow Big Gunpowder Falls upstream for about 0.7 mile along old Stockdale Road, then fork right uphill away from the river on the rutted dirt road. (The narrow footpath that continues along the river eventually crosses Sweathouse Branch and continues for a few hundred yards to Long Green Creek.)

Follow the wide path as it climbs obliquely along the side of the valley and curves to the right. Continue uphill to the rim of the valley. Pass through a pine plantation. Pass trails intersecting from either side. At a T-intersection, turn right to follow the main track, then turn left in 175 yards to continue on the main path.

As you approach two houses located on a gravel road, turn right back into the woods on a wide path starting next to a log cribbing. Continue through the woods on the wide path, passing obscure trails intersecting from either side. Eventually, after passing a pine plantation on the left, turn right at a T-intersection. Follow a wide path downhill as it curves left. Because this area is relatively unwooded and sunny, the trailside brush sometimes grows so rapidly that it obscures the path. When in doubt, plow straight ahead. (If you look closely, you will see traces of fences, gate-posts, and foundations indicating that this area was once a farmyard; the pine plantations occupy former fields.)

Follow the path to the right of a concrete-block shed, now in an advanced state of ruin. Thirty-five yards beyond the shed, fork right. Continue straight downhill with a pine plantation on your left, at one point passing a trail inter-secting from the left. At the bottom of the slope, follow the path as it curves left and climbs a small rise. Fifty-five yards past the top of the rise, turn right downhill onto a narrow and obscure footpath. Follow the footpath downhill and gradually to the right along the side of the ravine. (You can help to maintain this trail by breaking off twigs that grow out into the path.)

Eventually, cross a stream, then turn left onto the riverside trail. With the river on your right, follow the path to Belair Road.

16

GUNPOWDER FALLS STATE PARK

Belair Road Downstream

Walking and ski touring—5.0 or 7.0 miles (8.0 or 11.3 kilometers) round-trip, depending on whether you turn around at Philadelphia Road (Route 7) or at Pulaski Highway (Route 40). A footpath extends along the south bank of the river. Hike as far as you want and return the way you came. Although very attractive and easily passable, the trail is somewhat rough. Between Philadelphia Road and Pulaski Highway the landscape changes from Piedmont to Coastal Plain. The park is open daily from sunrise to sunset. Dogs must be leashed. Managed by the Maryland Park Service (telephone 592–2897).

THIS RIVERSIDE WALK passes the sites—and in a few cases, the relics—of some of the iron furnaces, forges, nail factories, and other industrial operations that were located along Big Gunpowder Falls above and below Philadelphia Road during the eighteenth and nineteenth centuries. The early ironworks needed water power just like any other mill. Low rock and wooden dams created a fall of water that turned a water wheel; through a series of gears and cams, the wheel operated the bellows for the smelting furnaces and forges, and also the mechanical hammers that beat the white-hot pig iron to remove impurities and to flatten it into plates and bars that could later be worked or cast into useful objects.

In 1719 Maryland's colonial legislature established a legal process to encourage the development of water power for the production of iron. The law stated in part: ". . . be it Enacted that if any person or persons shall desire to set up a forging mill or other convenience for carrying on Iron Works on land not before cultivated adjoining a stream, he may get a writ *ad quod dammum*"—that is, a writ of land condemnation. If the owner of the land refused to build a forge himself, the petitioner was granted a deed for one hundred acres, "the owner being paid for it." The law further provided: "If pig iron is not run in seven years, the grant is void." No fewer than twenty-three of these writs of private condemnation were granted between 1733 and 1767, most of which resulted in ironworks being built.

One forge site on Big Gunpowder Falls was the Long Calm, where Philadelphia Road used to ford the stream. (The Long Calm is located upstream from the present-day Interstate 95 bridge.) A forge was built here in 1757 by the Nottingham Company. Because the owners of the Nottingham Company were either British or Loyalists, their property was expropriated during the Revolution by the state Office of Confiscated Effects, whose ledgers show the site to have included "Forges, Sawmill, Gristmill, Forge Dam, Water Courses, and Many Improvements." In 1781 the state auctioned the Nottingham works to Charles Ridgely and Company. Under Ridgely's ownership the forge manufactured a variety of products, as indicated by a newspaper advertisement:

> Cannon (from Nine to Two-Pounders), Bar-Iron, pig iron, pots from 15 gallons to three quarts, kettles from 45 to 15 gallons; Dutch-ovens, tea-kettles, skillets, salt-pans, flat irons, mortars and pestles, wagon-boxes, stoves, dripping pans and bakers . . . N.B. Castings of any sort made on the shortest notice.

In 1795 Ridgely's Nottingham Forge burned to the ground, but was rebuilt. Forty years later, when David Ridgely tried unsuccessfully to sell the property, it was described in the advertisement as including a new dam and two forges, one new and the other built in 1827 for rolling hoops.

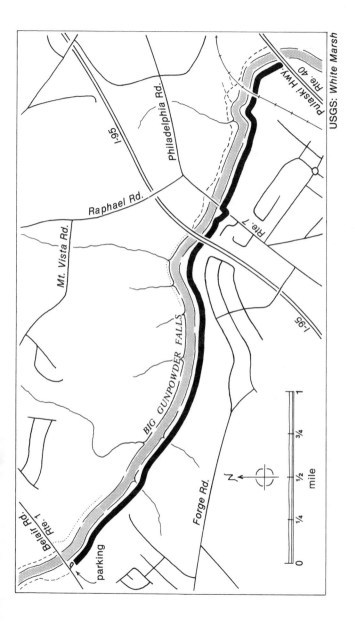

BIG GUNPOWDER FALLS

Pulaski Hwy. Rte. 40

Rte. 7

I-95

I-95

Raphael Rd.

Philadelphia Rd.

Mt. Vista Rd.

Belair Rd. Rte. 1

Forge Rd.

parking

N

0   1/4   1/2   3/4   1
         mile

By 1840 the plant was operated under lease by Horace Abbott and Company, which had a subcontract to make engine parts for the *Kamchatka,* a steam frigate being built in New York for the Russian navy. A reporter from the *American* visited the forges at the Long Calm and wrote:

> I proceeded to the other works on the Falls of the Great Gunpowder River, 14 miles from Baltimore near the Philadelphia Turnpike. This establishment was fitted up by these gentlemen for the purpose of making a heavier kind of work. The hammer which they have erected is driven by a powerful water wheel, 22 feet in diameter, with 14½-foot buckets, assisted by a fly wheel of 18 tons weight. There are two air furnaces besides several large fires for heating. When I was there, the workmen had just completed the main center shaft for the Russian steam frigate above alluded to. This shaft is the largest ever made in this country, being 14½ feet in length and 18½ inches in diameter, and is estimated to weigh *thirteen thousand* pounds.

In 1845 David Ridgely sold the forges at the Long Calm to Robert Howard, who the next year built an iron-smelting furnace farther downstream just west of Philadelphia Road. In 1856 this furnace produced 1100 tons of iron during thirty weeks of continuous blast. Two years later, however, Howard's forges and furnace on Big Gunpowder Falls were put out of operation permanently by a flood that destroyed the dam and cracked the furnace.

AUTOMOBILE: The section of Gunpowder Falls State Park explored by this walk is located northeast of Baltimore. The walk starts where Belair Road crosses Big Gunpowder Falls.

From Interstate 695 (the Beltway) northeast of Baltimore, take exit 32B for Route 1 north toward Bel Air. Follow Route 1 (Belair Road) about 5.4 miles to the bridge over Big Gunpowder Falls. A very small, obscure gravel parking area is located on the right side of the road just before the bridge, so be prepared to slow down and pull off the road.

WALK: From the south end of the bridge and with the river on your left, follow the footpath downstream through the woods and along the bank. Now and then the trail splits but soon rejoins. Continue on the riverside footpath downstream to the highway bridge at Interstate 95. Be alert for places where the path is being undermined by erosion.

Approximately 200 yards upstream from the Interstate 95 bridge, the path abruptly rises a few feet and passes above and to the right of the stone abutment of what was once a wooden dam. There is a matching abutment on the opposite bank. The dam supplied water to power Robert Howard's nineteenth-century ironworks at the Long Calm.

Continue under the Interstate 95 bridge, then follow the path toward another bridge at Philadelphia Road (Route 7). About 100 yards before reaching Philadelphia Road, the path veers to the right away from the water up to a lawn by a tavern and oyster house. Follow the edge of the lawn to Philadelphia Road.

A bridge—the Forges Bridge—was first built here in 1822, a few years after Philadelphia Road itself was moved from the ford at the Long Calm.

If you wish to continue downstream, turn left toward the bridge, then cross Philadelphia Road and pass a gate. With the river on your left, continue downstream on a paved road, which eventually ends at a place where the pavement spreads out in a clearing. A gravel bar below this spot is a good place to stop (although the path continues downstream 0.2 mile under the B&O bridge to Route 40).

As just noted, south of the present-day Philadelphia Road bridge, the asphalt path leads 0.5 mile to a circular clearing. This was the site of the Joppa Iron Works, also known as Big

Mills or Patterson's Iron Works. The works were constructed in 1817, and by 1820 fifteen men and six boys were employed producing sheet iron, barrel hoops, spikes, cut nails, and brads. By 1850, the Patterson Iron Works employed 130 hands producing 36,000 kegs of nails per year. The following year the works was rebuilt on a far larger scale to include six puddling furnaces, one heating furnace, one water-driven hammer, two trains of rolls to produce sheet iron, and thirty-seven nail machines to cut nails from the sheets. The works continued in operation until the 1860s, after which they were dismantled. In 1913 a distillery was built on the old ironworks foundations. The distillery building survived until the property was acquired for park purposes in 1970.

On the opposite bank of the river, a small cut-stone furnace is built into a cleft in the rock back a few dozen yards from the river's edge next to the rapids. At low water, the site of a former dam or bridge is marked by a row of twisted iron spikes sunk in the river bed just above the rapids. These rapids, incidentally, are the last on Big Gunpowder Falls and mark as well as any other point in the fall line zone the transition from the Piedmont to the Coastal Plain. If you continue downstream to Route 40, notice the marked difference in landscape farther down the river.

Return to Belair Road the way you came. There is also a path of sorts along the north bank, but it is obscure and overgrown.

17

FORT HOWARD PARK

Walking—1.0 mile (1.6 kilometers). Explore the waterfront fortifications at the tip of North Point, from which there are sweeping views east over Chesapeake Bay, south across the mouth of the Patapsco River, and west to Sparrows Point. The park opens daily at 9 AM and closes at hours that correspond approximately with daylight. Dogs must be leashed. Managed by the Baltimore County Department of Recreation and Parks (telephone 477–8330).

LIKE MAYAN RUINS overrun by jungle, several massive structures lie half-buried in the tangled brush and woods at the tip of North Point. All are of concrete, empty, strangely abstract like the imaginary buildings in the drawings of M. C. Escher. These are the bunkers and huge amphitheater-like gun pits of Fort Howard, which during the first two decades of this century helped to guard the water approach to Baltimore.

Built at the end of the nineteenth century during the Spanish-American War, Fort Howard never saw combat then, nor did it during World War I, when Forts Smallwood, Armistead, and Howard formed Baltimore's line of coastal defense against attacks that never came. The Fort Howard garrison, however, was said to maintain a high standard of proficiency. *The Baltimore Sun* of October 14, 1908, reported that the Howard gunners had been credited with setting a world's record for accuracy by hitting, nine times out of ten, a target that was being towed in the shipping channel nearly three miles away. The fort's guns included two batteries of twelve-inch mortars that

fired projectiles weighing 1000 pounds. The mortars were housed in the largest firing pits. Another emplacement held two twelve-inch disappearing rifles (i.e., modern rifled cannon—not smoothbore) that were raised for firing and lowered behind the revetment walls for loading. Four other emplacements (only three of which survive) housed six-inch, five-inch, and 4.7-inch rifles and three-inch rapid-fire guns.

In 1941, long after the guns had been removed, the fort was decommissioned as obsolete. The bunkers, barracks, officers' houses, and grounds were turned over to the Veterans Administration for development of the present-day hospital. Twenty-five years later, the area occupied by the concrete revetments was returned to the Army for use by the intelligence school at Fort Holabird. During the Vietnam War, a mock Vietnamese village was constructed in the underbrush and vines among the old coastal batteries.

When Fort Holabird was closed in 1972, its 62-acre parcel at North Point was deeded to Baltimore County by the General Services Administration under the federal government's Legacy of Parks program, by which surplus federal property is donated to local governments with the provision that the land be used for recreation. The hospital grounds, however, are not part of the park and are not open to visitors.

North Point is where four thousand English troops landed in the fall of 1814 for their abortive march on Baltimore. Major General Robert Ross, commander of the British army, had announced his intention to use Baltimore—that "nest of privateers"—as his headquarters during the coming winter. He said that with the city as his base, his army would go where it pleased through Maryland.

Two years previously, the youthful United States had declared war on England. In a petition to President Jefferson, Baltimore had urged war with France, also, on the grounds that her conduct was "scarcely less atrocious than that of England." Since 1793 England and France, at that time the world's two most powerful nations, had been locked in a protracted global war, and both countries regularly confiscated American mer-

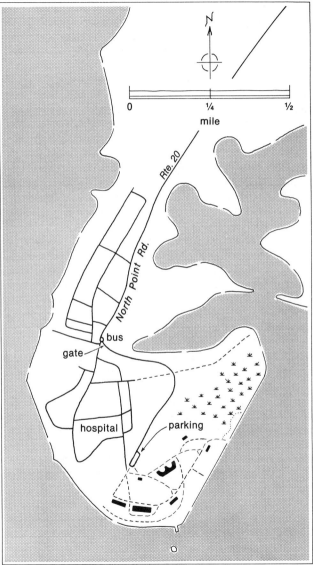

N

0   1/4   1/2
mile

Rte. 20

North Point Rd.

bus

gate

hospital

parking

USGS: *Sparrows Point*

chant ships and cargoes in an attempt to prevent supplies from reaching the enemy. The United States itself engaged in the same practice during the Civil War, but in the early 1800s most Americans saw the seizures as a piratical violation of their neutral rights.

Ire toward England was intensified starting in 1805 by the British navy's practice of stopping passenger vessels in United States coastal waters and removing all sailors whom the English surmised to be British subjects, for the Royal Navy was sorely in need of seamen. Also, the "war hawks," a group of congressmen from the frontier states, openly urged that war with Great Britain would enable the United States to seize Canada and its lucrative fur trade, to end the Indian menace in the Ohio Valley (where massacres and conspiracies were said to be incited by British agents), and to throw open more western land for settlement.

The war, however, did not go as planned. Successive attempts to invade Canada failed miserably. At Baltimore, the British blockade of Chesapeake Bay reduced the export trade to almost nothing. Among shipowners, only the privateersmen made substantial profits through the seizure and sale of English merchant ships. Commissioned by the federal government as private warships, Baltimore's privateers captured about a third of all enemy vessels that were taken during the war. After being seized, the ships were sailed to American ports, where they and their cargoes were sold through judicial condemnation by admiralty courts.

In the spring of 1814, Great Britain and its allies finally forced the abdication of Napoleon. England then turned its attention to the United States. The London newspapers announced that an expeditionary force of seasoned troops and sailors was being readied. "The seat of the American government, but more particularly Baltimore, is to be the immediate object of attack. . . . Terms will be offered to the American government at the point of the bayonet."

In mid-August the British force appeared in Chesapeake Bay. Baltimore gained time while the English marched from the Patuxent River to Washington, which they captured on August 24, 1814. This event was enormously exaggerated in England, where the brief occupation of the national capital—a straggling, swampy place of 8000 inhabitants—was touted by the British press to be equivalent to the fall of London. *The Times* of London declared, "The world is speedily to be delivered of the mischievous example of the existence of a government founded on democratic rebellion."

After only one day in Washington, where they burned the government buildings, the "modern Goths"—as one indignant American writer called the British—marched back to their ships. The armada sailed off down the Chesapeake, perhaps in an effort to lull Baltimore into thinking that the danger had passed, but the British soon turned northward.

Meanwhile, Baltimore dug in. The previous year a half-million dollars had been raised by subscription among the residents for the defense of the city because no aid came from Washington. Fort McHenry had been strengthened and other shore batteries constructed. A line of earthworks over a mile long was thrown up to the east of the city at Hampstead Hill, across land now occupied by Patterson Park and Johns Hopkins Hospital. This was to be the main line of resistance.

Work on the fortifications continued until Sunday, September 11, when three alarm guns in the courthouse square and the ringing of bells announced the arrival of the British squadron of fifty ships at North Point, fourteen miles east of Baltimore at the mouth of the Patapsco River. After the militia had mustered, Major General Samuel Smith, to whom the city had assigned its defense, sent General John Stricker with 3185 men out Philadelphia Road to reconnoiter and to delay the enemy's advance. By that evening Stricker had reached the narrow neck of land between the head of Bear Creek and the Back River, about halfway between Baltimore and North Point. He deployed his men there, except for a contingent of cavalry and riflemen who were sent farther ahead toward a farm owned by Robert Gorsuch.

At three o'clock the following morning, four thousand British soldiers rowed ashore in the dark at North Point. Their landing place at the tip of the peninsula was chosen because the Patapsco was thought to be too shallow for the larger ships to go farther upstream. The battle plan called for the smaller boats to push past Fort McHenry and to attack the city at the same time as the assault by land.

As light came on, the British army advanced up North Point Road toward Baltimore. Eventually they stopped to rest while General Ross and his retinue left the road in order to get something to eat at the Gorsuch farm. According to Robert Gorsuch's grandson, the elder Gorsuch was forced not only to provide breakfast for the General and eight officers but also to eat and drink a sample of every dish that he served before the British would touch it. Talking of the coming battle while he ate, General Ross purportedly boasted that he would "eat his supper in Baltimore, or in Hell."

Meanwhile, John Stricker (according to his account of the 12th of September) learned from his horse scouts that "the enemy in small force was enjoying itself at Gorsuch's farm." Two hundred and thirty infantry, some cavalry, and a cannon were immediately pushed forward. Stricker reported:

> This small volunteer corps had proceeded scarcely half a mile before the main body of the enemy showed itself, which was immediately attacked. The infantry and riflemen maintained a fire of some minutes and returned with some loss in killed and wounded; the cavalry and artillery, owing to the disadvantageous ground, not being able to support them.

The skirmish was more critical than the Americans thought. On the British side, an eyewitness account was provided by the Reverend Mr. Gleig, the military chaplain. He had been waiting with the main British force while General Ross breakfasted at the Gorsuch farm. After an hour the troops started to move again, but they had not traveled more than a mile when the "sharp fire of musketry was heard in front, and shortly afterward a mounted officer came galloping to the rear, who desired us to quicken our pace for that the advance guard was engaged." Gleig continued:

> At this intelligence the ranks closed, and the troops advanced at a brisk rate, and in profound silence. The firing still continued, though from its running and irregular sound, it promised little else than a skirmish; but whether it was kept up by detached parties alone, or by the outposts of a regular army, we could not tell because, from the quantity of wood with which the country abounded, and the total absence of all hills or eminences, it was impossible to discern what was going on at the distance of half a mile from the spot where we stood.
>
> We were already drawing near the scene of action, when another officer came at full speed toward us, with horror and dismay in his countenance, and calling loudly for a surgeon. Every man felt within himself that all was not right, though none was willing to believe the whispers of his own terror. But what at first we would not guess at, because we dreaded it so much, was soon realized; for the aide-de-camp had scarcely passed when the General's horse, without its rider, and with the saddle and housing stained with blood, came plunging onwards. In a few moments we reached the ground where the skirmishing had taken place, and beheld General Ross laid by the side of the road, under a canopy of blankets, and apparently in the agonies of death. As soon as the firing began he had ridden to the front, that he might ascertain from whence it originated and, mingling with the skirmishers, was shot in the side by a rifleman. The wound was mortal; he fell into the arms of his aide-de-camp, and lived only long enough to name his wife, and to commend his family to the protection of his country. He was removed towards the fleet, but expired before his bearers could reach the boat.
>
> It is impossible to conceive the effect which this melancholy spectacle produced throughout the army . . . . All eyes were turned upon him as we passed, and a sort of involuntary groan ran from rank to rank from the front to the rear of the column.

Nonetheless, the British pushed on until they ran into General Stricker's main force. A battle of an hour and a half followed. As the British troops advanced at a walking pace, the

Americans fired what Gleig described as a "dreadful discharge of grape and canister shot, of old locks, pieces of broken muskets, and everything which they could cram into their guns." After firing one volley, part of the American line retreated without orders. As the lines of British approached nearer and nearer, firing as they came, General Stricker was forced to pull his troops back to the main line of fortifications outside the city.

The next day, after a bivouac at the North Point battlefield, the British continued slowly toward Baltimore, hindered by the trees which the retreating Americans had cut down across the road during the night. Rain fell all day and it was not until evening that the British covered the seven miles to Hampstead Hill, where they stopped in front of the American fortifications. Gleig reported:

> It now appeared that the corps which we had beaten yesterday was only a detachment, and not a large one, from the force collected for the defense of Baltimore . . . . Upon a ridge of hills which concealed the town itself from observation stood the grand army, consisting of twenty thousand men. Not trusting to his superiority in numbers, their general had there entrenched them in the most formidable manner, having covered the whole face of the heights with breastworks, thrown back his left so as to rest it upon a strong fort, erected for the protection of the river, and constructed a chain of field redoubts which covered his right and commanded the entire ascent. Along the line of the hill were likewise fleches and other projecting works, from which a cross fire might be kept up; and there were mounted throughout this commanding position no less than one hundred pieces of cannon.

The new British commander, Colonel Arthur Brooke, tried to outflank the defenses by moving his troops to the north, but the Americans kept between the British and the city. Brooke then decided to try a night attack, provided he could receive support from the navy. But, as reflected in our national anthem, the English ships were repulsed at Fort McHenry, and Brooke eventually determined that attack was futile. In the early morning, while their ships continued the unsuccessful attack on Fort

McHenry, the British began their retreat, which was not discovered by the Americans until daylight. The American troops were so worn out from the two days of watching and waiting, much of it in the rain, that General Smith decided not to counterattack. By the next day, the British had returned to their ships and were gone.

After the retreat, the Baltimore newspapers dubbed the British the "night-retrograders." In England, however, *The Times* of London described the repulse at Baltimore and the contemporaneous naval defeat of the British at Plattsburg on Lake Champlain as a "lamentable event to the civilized world."

BUS: North Point is served by the MTA Fort Howard bus (#4) that for part of its route follows Dundalk Avenue south from Holabird Avenue. From downtown Baltimore, Dundalk Avenue can be reached by bus #10 or bus #20, from which you can transfer to bus #4 at the intersection of Holabird Avenue and Dundalk Avenue. Ride bus #4 all the way through Sparrows Point to the end of the line at the entrance to the Fort Howard Veterans Hospital. From the bus stop, enter the park through the left gate. Follow the winding drive to the parking lot. Be alert for automobiles; walk on the road's left shoulder to minimize the risk of being hit by a car approaching from behind.

AUTOMOBILE: Fort Howard Park is located southeast of Baltimore at the tip of North Point, where the Patapsco River joins Chesapeake Bay.

From Interstate 695 (the Beltway) southeast of Baltimore, take exit 41 for Cove Road toward Route 20 (and Route 151). Follow Cove Road to an intersection with Route 151 at a traffic light, then turn left onto Route 151 south. Follow Route 151 south 2.2 miles, then bear left onto Route 20 south toward Edgemere and Fort Howard; this intersection is poorly marked and occurs at a yield sign just before Route 151 passes under the Interstate 695 bridge.

Follow Route 20 south 4.0 miles to the entrance to Fort Howard Veterans Hospital and (just to the left) the entrance to Fort Howard Park. Fork left for the park and follow the curving drive to the parking lot at the end of the road.

WALK: From the parking lot, follow any of several paths that lead to the various gun emplacements and to the water's edge. Fort Howard is so small that you can easily explore the entire installation of scattered gun sites.

18

CYLBURN ARBORETUM

Walking—1.0 mile (1.6 kilometers). The old Tyson estate, with its Victorian stone mansion, formal gardens, and extensive woods, is now Baltimore City's arboretum and horticulture center. Labels identify hundreds of varieties of trees, shrubs, flowers, and other plants. Over 150 species of birds have been seen here. The arboretum is open daily from sunrise to sunset. Dogs are prohibited. Managed by the Baltimore City Department of Recreation and Parks (telephone 396–0180).

SUMPTUOUS CYLBURN ARBORETUM occupies 170 acres of meadows and woods on a high plateau above Jones Falls Valley north of Coldspring New Town and south of Northern Parkway. A wide path follows the top of the bluff around three sides of the park and ends at the formal gardens behind the Cylburn Mansion.

Started in 1863, Cylburn was developed during the decade following the Civil War as the country estate of Jesse Tyson, the son of Isaac Tyson, Jr., Baltimore's chrome king. The gray stone for the mansion was quarried at the Bare Hills west of Lake Roland, where the Tysons had some of their chromite and copper mines.

In 1888 Jesse Tyson married Edith Johns, a Baltimore debutante who in later years Alfred Jenkins Shriver listed in his will as among the ten most beautiful Baltimore women of his era (and all of whom, therefore, were by his testamentary directions painted together in a mural at Johns Hopkins University's

Shriver Hall—each woman "at the height of her beauty"). The Tysons entertained frequently and lavishly at Cylburn, where they, their servants, and weekend guests arrived and departed by the Northern Central Railroad; a private carriage road ran from the mansion to the Cylburn station, located off what was then Belvedere Avenue. Four years after Tyson's death in 1906, his widow married Lieutenant (later Major) Bruce Cotton, and for decades Cylburn continued to be a showplace where Baltimore society gathered for receptions in the large drawing room or wandered the lawns and gardens that were lit with hundreds of Japanese lanterns during summer musicales. Following Mrs. Cotton's death in 1942, Major Cotton sold the property to the city for a low price with the specific intention that the estate be made a city park.

If you want to learn to identify trees, the large variety of labeled specimens at Cylburn Arboretum provides excellent practice and an enjoyable excursion at all times of year. Oak, hickory, and tulip trees (also called yellow poplar) and to a lesser extent maple, beech, and ash dominate the scene, as is typical in eastern Maryland. Dogwood, sassafras, and mountain laurel are also widespread in the understory.

Learning to identify trees is not difficult. Every walk or automobile trip is an opportunity for practice. Notice the overall forms and branching habits of the trees, and also the distinctive qualities of their twigs, buds, bark, leaves, flowers, and fruits or seeds. These factors are the key identification features that distinguish one species from another. Finally, when using a field guide, check the maps or descriptions that delineate the geographic range within which the tree or shrub is likely to be found.

Some trees, of course, have very distinctive and reliable forms. Familiar evergreens like balsam fir and eastern red cedar have a conical shape, like a dunce cap, although in dense stands the red cedar tapers very little and assumes the columnar form of the Italian cypress, which it somewhat resembles. The deciduous little-leaf linden, imported from Europe and used as

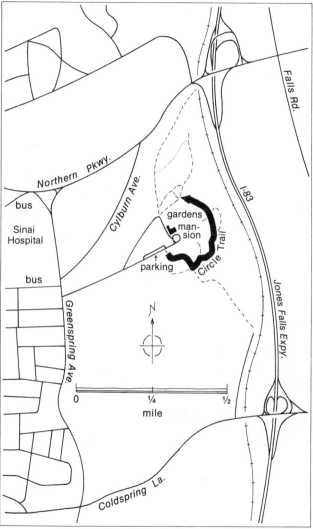

USGS: *Baltimore West*

a street tree, is also more or less conical in shape. The elm displays a spreading form like a head of broccoli. A full-bodied egg-shape is characteristic of the sugar maple and beech, although both will develop long, branchless trunks in crowded woods, as do most forest trees competing for light. The vertically exaggerated cigar shape of Lombardy poplar—a form called fastigiate—and the pendulous, trailing quality of weeping willow are unmistakable. (Both Lombardy poplar and weeping willow have been introduced to North America from abroad.)

Branching habit, an important clue to some trees, is observable even at a distance. White pine, for example, has markedly horizontal branches with a slight upward tilt at the tips, like a hand turned with its palm up. Norway spruce (another imported species) is usually seen as an ornamental tree dwarfing and darkening a house near which it was planted fifty or a hundred years ago; it is a very tall evergreen with long, evenly spaced, drooping lower branches. The slender lower branches of pin oak slant downward, while those of white oak and red oak are often massive and horizontal, especially on trees growing in the open. The lower branches of the horse chestnut (yet another European import) also droop but then curl up at the tips in chunky twigs. Elm branches spread up and out like the mouth of a trumpet. The trunk of the mature honeylocust diverges into large branches somewhat in the manner of an elm.

A good botanist or forester can identify trees by their twigs alone—that is, by the end portion of the branch that constitutes the newest growth. During winter the shape, color, size, position, and sheathing of buds are important. For instance, beech buds are long and pointed, tan, and sheathed with overlapping scales like shingles. Sycamore and magnolia buds are wrapped in a single scale. The twigs of horse chestnut are tipped with a big, sticky, brown bud, while those of silver maple, and to a lesser extent red maple, end with large clusters of red buds. Some oaks, such as white oak, have hairless terminal buds, while other species, such as black oak, have hairy end buds.

Aside from buds, other characteristics of twigs are color, thorns, hair, pith, and the size, shape, and position of leaf scars marking where the leaf stems were attached. For example, most maple twigs are reddish brown, but the twigs of striped maple and mountain maple are greenish. Thorns and spines are significant because relatively few trees have them, notably honeylocust, black locust, Hercules club, prickly ash, buckthorn bumelia, devil's walking stick, Osage-orange, American plum, some crab apples, and the many varieties of hawthorn. Most oaks have hairless twigs, although some species such as blackjack oak are distinctly hairy. As for pith, it can be chambered, solid, spongy, or of different colors, depending on the species. It was noted earlier that oak, hickory, and tulip trees are common forest species near Baltimore, but only the pith of white oak in cross section forms a star. Finally, the location of leaf scars in opposite pairs along the twigs (as with maples) distinguishes a wide variety of trees and shrubs from those with leaf scars arranged alternately, first on one side and then on the other (as with oaks). All these distinguishing features can best be appreciated simply by examining the twigs of different species.

Bark is not always a reliable clue for identifying trees, as the color and texture of bark change with age or from trunk to branches to twigs. Often the distinctive character of bark is seen only in the trunks of large, mature trees. Bark can be smooth, furrowed, scaly, plated, shaggy, fibrous, crisscrossed, corky, or papery. Some trees, of course, may be clearly identified by their bark. The names *shagbark hickory* and *paper birch* speak for themselves. Striped maple has longitudinal, whitish stripes in the smooth green bark of the younger trees. The crisscrossed ridges of white ash, the light blotches on sycamores, and the smooth gray skin of beech are equally distinctive. Birches and some cherries are characterized by horizontal lenticels like random dashes.

Most people notice leaves, particularly their shape. The leaves of the gray birch are triangular; catalpa, heart-shaped;

sweetgum, star-shaped; beech, elliptical (or actually pointed at each end); and black willow narrower still and thus lanceolate. Notice also the leaf margin or edge. Is it smooth like rhododendron, wavy like water oak, serrated like basswood, or deeply lobed like most maples? And how many lobes are there? Tulip trees, for example, have easily recognized four-lobed leaves; maples have three- or five-lobed leaves. Also, are the lobe tips rounded like white oak or pointed like red oak? Or, maybe, as with sassafras and red mulberry, the same tree has leaves that are shaped differently, the most distinctive being those with a single asymmetrical lobe creating a leaf outline like a mitten.

Some leaves such as those of the Japanese maple, horse chestnut, and Ohio buckeye are palmately compound, meaning that they are actually composed of leaflets radiating from the end of the stem like fingers from the palm. In the fall the whole compound leaf drops off the tree as a unit. Other leaves, such as ash, hickory, and sumac, are pinnately compound, being composed of leaflets arranged in opposite pairs along a central stalk. Still other leaves are bipinnately compound, somewhat like a fern. The leaflets grow from stalks that, in turn, spread from a central stalk. Honeylocust, Kentucky coffeetree, and the ornamental imported silktree are examples.

Although the needles of evergreens are not as varied as the leaves of deciduous plants, there are still several major points to look for, such as the number of needles grouped together. White pine has fascicles of five; pitchpine, loblolly pine, and sometimes shortleaf pine have fascicles of three; and jack pine, red pine, Virginia pine, Austrian pine, and sometimes shortleaf pine have fascicles of two. Needles of spruce, hemlock, and fir grow singly, but are joined to the twig in distinctive ways. Spruce needles grow from little woody pegs, hemlock needles from smaller bumps, and fir needles directly from the twig, leaving a rounded pit when pulled off. Spruce needles tend to be four-sided, hemlock flat, and fir somewhere in between. The needles of larch (also called tamarack) grow in dense clusters and all drop off in winter.

Flowers are a spectacular, though short-lived, feature of some trees and shrubs. Three variables are color, form, and (less reliably) time of bloom. Eastern redbud, with red-purple clusters, and shadbush (also called Allegheny serviceberry), with small, white, five-petaled flowers, are among the first of our native trees to bloom, sometimes as early as late March in the Baltimore region. As members of the rose family, apples, cherries, plums, peaches, and hawthorns all have flowers with five petals (usually pink or white) in loose clusters, typically blooming in April. The blossoms of flowering dogwood (also appearing in April or early May) consist of four white, petal-like bracts, each with a brown notch at the tip, while the flowers of alternate-leaf dogwood consist of loose, white clusters. These are a few of our native species commonly thought of as flowering trees and shrubs, but the blossoms of other native species are equally distinctive, such as the small but numerous flowers of maples or the tuliplike flowers and durable husks of tulip trees. Unlike most trees, witch hazel, which produces small, yellow, scraggly flowers, blooms in fall or winter.

Finally, the seeds or fruit of a tree are a conspicuous element in summer and fall, sometimes lasting into winter and even spring. Nobody who sees a tree with acorns could fail to know that it is an oak, although some varieties, such as willow oak and shingle oak (also know as northern laurel oak) are deceptive. Distinctive nuts are also produced by beech trees, horse chestnuts, hickories, and walnuts. Some seeds, like ash and maple, have wings. Others, such as honeylocust, Kentucky coffeetree, and redbud, come in pods like beans and in fact are members of the same general legume family. The seeds of birches, poplars, and willows hang in tassels, while those of sweetgum and sycamore form prickle-balls (as do the shells of horse chestnut and buckeye). Eastern cottonwood produces seeds that are windborne by cottonlike tufts. And, of course, brightly colored berries and fruits are produced by many species, such as crabapples, holly, hawthorn, and hackberry. Among needle evergreens, spruce and pine cones hang from the twigs, while fir cones stand upright, and the small hemlock cones grow from the twig tips.

BUS: From downtown Baltimore take MTA bus #19 via Eutaw Street, North Avenue, and Garrison Boulevard to the intersection of Greenspring and Cylburn avenues. You will know that your stop is coming when the bus passes Sinai Hospital and turns uphill from Belvedere Avenue onto Greenspring Avenue. MTA bus #1 also runs to Greenspring and Cylburn avenues. Yet another bus—MTA bus #44—passes a short distance north of the entrance to the arboretum, which is within sight of the intersection of Greenspring and Cylburn avenues.

AUTOMOBILE: Cylburn Arboretum is located in north Baltimore. The entrance is on the east side of Greenspring Avenue 0.3 mile south of Northern Parkway and 0.7 mile north of Coldspring Lane, both of which can be reached by exits off Interstate 83 (Jones Falls Expressway) inside the Beltway.

From Interstate 83 inside the Beltway, take the exit for Northern Parkway westbound. Follow Northern Parkway west 0.3 mile, then turn left onto Cylburn Avenue. Follow Cylburn Avenue uphill 0.5 mile to Greenspring Avenue. Turn left onto Greenspring Avenue, then turn immediately left again into Cylburn Arboretum.

WALK: Start your walk on the rutted gravel road descending from the entrance drive opposite some parking bays for cars and buses. (As of 1987, this spot was located about 100 yards before the entrance road reaches the circular drive in front of the mansion, but the configuration of roads and parking lots may be changed.)

Follow the gravel road downhill and into the woods. As you enter the woods, watch for a wide footpath (the Circle Trail) on your left. Turn left onto the Circle Trail and follow it along the rim of the bluff. After about 125 yards, turn right to continue on the Circle Trail, which eventually brings you around to the rear of the mansion, where you can explore the various specialty gardens.

19

GWYNNS FALLS PARK

Walking and ski touring—3.0 miles (4.8 kilometers). A winding path follows the side of Gwynns Falls Valley, with views out over the stream to the opposing hillsides. Return along the bottomland. The park is open daily from sunrise to sunset. Dogs must be leashed. Managed by the Baltimore City Department of Recreation and Parks (telephone 396–0010).

GWYNNS FALLS PARK is the eastern, older half of Baltimore's largest park complex. The other half is Leakin Park. Totaling about 1120 acres, these two adjacent parks include the steep valleys of Gwynns Falls and its tributary Dead Run at the western edge of the city. Together they are Baltimore's principal "wilderness" reservation. Here it is possible to take a walk in a forest of immense oak, hickory, ash, sycamore, beech, and tulip trees entirely within the city limits.

The route described at the end of the chapter follows the millrace path, so-called because it is, indeed, part of an old millrace that was filled in to form a walkway. In a photograph from 1915, the millrace path is shown as a beautifully groomed promenade about fifteen feet wide. Prior to its conversion to a path, the race ran from a dam near Dickeyville downstream along the side of the valley to a site near the present-day Edmondson Avenue bridge, where during the nineteenth century there was a complex of grist mills called Calverton Mills or Five Mills. Farther downstream, the Ellicotts had a group of three flour mills near Frederick Road, to which water was fed by a race that started below Calverton Mills. Other mills were

established farther upstream, notably the Powhatan Woolen Mills near Woodlawn, the Ashland Mills at present-day Dickeyville, and a grist mill at Franklintown. Overlooking the valleys of Gwynns Falls and Dead Run were the nineteenth-century estates and mansions of some of Baltimore's most wealthy citizens.

In 1904 the Olmstead Brothers, Boston's pre-eminent land planning firm and consultants to many eastern cities, presented their *Report upon the Development of Public Grounds for Greater Baltimore*. The Olmstead report recommended that the city develop a comprehensive park system based on stream valleys and adjacent lands, as has since been done at Gwynns Falls, Herring Run, Stony Run, and to a lesser extent at other streams within the city. Gradually Gwynns Falls Park and Leakin Park have been pieced together by a series of purchases made between 1904 and the present. The last major acquisition was in 1969, when the 100-acre Windsor estate on Windsor Mill and Wetheredsville roads was purchased; a few more acres have been added from time to time since then.

During the 1960s and '70s, the big parks at Gwynns Falls and Dead Run were in danger of decimation. Protracted public debate culminated in a squall of litigation to bar use of the parks as an expressway route for the extension of Interstate 70 eastward into Baltimore. For those interested in the survival of urban parklands, the episode makes an enlightening case history.

The origins of the highway/park saga date back to the early 1940s, when planners for the city first raised the possibility of a crosstown expressway to replace Route 40, at that time a major interstate road. In the 1950s and early '60s, the Harbor Tunnel Thruway and most of the Beltway were built, carrying interstate traffic around the city while yet providing highway access to Baltimore's port area and industrial southeastern sector. Planning and more planning continued, however, for an east-west expressway somewhere through the middle of Baltimore.

In 1962 a city-wide hearing was held at Eastern High School

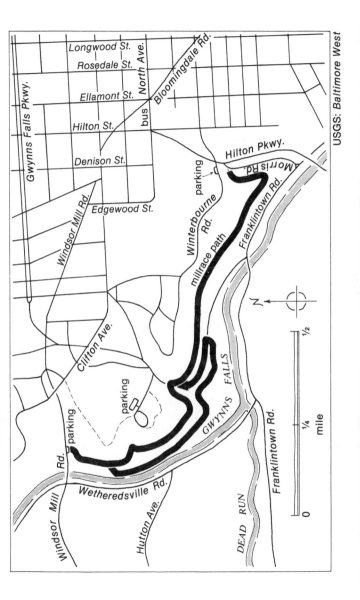

USGS: Baltimore West

on the recommended alignment for the entire inner-city highway system, consisting of Interstate 70, Interstate 95, and Interstate 83. When the discussion turned to the segment of Interstate 70 through Gwynns Falls and Leakin parks, many park users and nearby residents opposed the highway altogether while others urged that if it were built, it should be put along the *northern* side of the parks (farther from their homes). After still further study by the highway consultants, a mayoral committee, and yet another planning firm, the city determined in 1965 that the more northerly alignment through the parks was least objectionable. In February 1967 the northern park route received final approval by the federal government, which was to pay 90 percent of the highway's cost.

Even so, still more study and hearings were conducted during the following years as plans for the city's expressway system were revised and refined by a "concept team" of engineers, landscape architects, sociologists, economists, and other consultants whose interdisciplinary approach received considerable attention in national planning circles. The result was an alignment for Interstate 70 that would pass through Leakin and Gwynns Falls parks, curve southward to connect with the Franklin-Mulberry corridor, and then continue still farther south to link with Interstate 95 west of Carroll Park.

At a "design hearing" in May 1971, the plan for the segment of Interstate 70 through Leakin and Gwynns Falls parks indicated that about 130 acres (12 percent of the park complex) would be taken by the highway itself. The eight-lane expressway would slice through the Crimea section of Leakin Park in a trench that would be covered for part of its length, would follow the crest of the ridge between the valleys of Gwynns Falls and Dead Run to the confluence of the two streams, would cross the central valley on a long, high bridge, and from there would run through the middle of Gwynns Falls Park to the Franklin-Mulberry spur and Interstate 95.

To reduce neighborhood opposition and to compensate for what everyone acknowledged would be severe damage to the parks, the plan featured a variety of new recreational facilities, including a year-round day camp, three new swimming pools, more than thirty tennis courts, and several new ballfields at intervals around the rim of the valleys, as well as an extensively refurbished trail system and the clearing or thinning of trees and brush from three hundred acres. The planners' report said that this program of recreational development would restore the remaining parkland to the functional equivalent of a park without a highway, but many opponents saw the proposal simply as a further degradation of the unique wilderness character of the park. Other neighborhood groups who had little use for the passive character of the park liked the recreational improvements but for the most part still opposed the highway. Nor did anyone have a solution to the inexorable fact that the proposed recreational improvements would quickly deteriorate because of Baltimore's well-documented inability to pay for maintenance of more than a very limited number of such facilities. Meanwhile, implementation of the plan for added recreational facilities was made a major condition for federal financing of the highway under 4(f) of the Department of Transportation Act of 1966, which requires "all possible planning to minimize harm" to public parks.

In 1971 the highway controversy flared into litigation. Opponents of the park route brought a series of suits against city, state, and federal officials to bar acquisition of the right-of-way and to prevent construction. The principal case was filed against Secretary of Transportation John Volpe and other officials by the Sierra Club and a corporation calling itself Volunteers Opposing Leakin Park Expressway (V.O.L.P.E., Inc.). The Sierra Club's complaint alleged many procedural and substantive flaws in the highway planning process, but the court focused on the limited issue of whether the various public hearings concerning the placement of Interstate 70 through Leakin and Gwynns Falls parks satisfied federal requirements. Stating that a major purpose of a "location hearing" is to present for public comment alternative alignments for the highway, the court noted that at the 1962 hearing only one route—the southern route—had been proposed through Leakin Park. This route had later been rejected in favor of the northern park alignment, which the court said had never been presented with or without alternatives at a hearing intended to elicit comments on the highway's location. In consequence, federal approval was voided and another location hearing was required to be held. This was done in December 1972, six months after the court's decision.

At the new hearing so many people wanted to speak that the meeting had to be continued for three additional evenings. Representatives of local business organizations favored the park highway, as they always had. Area residents, however, were nearly unanimous in their opposition to all eight alternative routes that were presented, although some speakers urged that the park be developed for active recreation. Following the hearing, city and state agencies again approved the northern park route.

In a second highway suit decided in 1973, the park plaintiffs joined another anti-expressway coalition (M.A.D.,Inc., standing for Movement Against Destruction) to stop work on the Franklin-Mulberry spur—now designated Interstate 170—until an environmental impact statement under the National Environmental Policy Act of 1969 had been prepared for the entire interrelated highway system. Because the western end of the Franklin-Mulberry highway was planned to join Interstate 70, the park plaintiffs feared that the vast expense of the Franklin-Mulberry project (more than $100 million) would become justification for construction of the park highway as well, even though the environmental effects of Interstate 70 had not been evaluated when the Franklin-Mulberry spur was approved. The court ruled, however, that the Franklin-Mulberry highway was not so interrelated to the other expressway segments that the whole system needed to be evaluated together. And, indeed, the Franklin-Mulberry highway, which is less than 1½ miles long, now exists by itself, corresponding to the spur of Interstate 70 stretching from the Beltway eastward to its abrupt termination at the western boundary of Leakin Park.

After the spate of litigation in the early 1970s, planning for the park segment of Interstate 70 continued for a period, but then slowed and in most respects stopped. In a tentative agreement reached in 1974, the Federal Highway Administration undertook to pay for the proposed recreational development of the parks as an integral part of highway construction, if the Secretary of Transportation were to approve the project again. A revised and expanded environmental impact statement—prepared in draft form for the 1972 hearing—was completed in 1975 but never released. Nor was the project again submitted for federal review, so low was its priority compared to other local highway and boulevard projects.

In other developments, leaders of Baltimore's business community, who for years had urged that the park highway was needed as a link in the truck route between the port and the Midwest, changed their opinion, concluding that Interstate 95 and the Beltway provided adequate access to Interstate 70 west of the city, and that the central business district might be better served by other transit projects.

As of 1987, plans to extend Interstate 70 eastward through Gwynns Falls and Leakin parks had been completely abandoned. During the early 1980s, federal funds originally earmarked for the park segment of Interstate 70 were spent on other local road and bridge projects. The city has even undertaken to sell the right-of-way that it acquired between the western end of the Franklin-Mulberry corridor and the unfinished interchange on Interstate 95 near Caton Avenue. However, as development intensifies to the west of Baltimore, proposals to extend Interstate 70 into the city will almost certainly be revived.

BUS: This walk starts near the west end of North Avenue. Coming from the east, take MTA bus #13 via North Avenue; from downtown take MTA bus #19 via Eutaw and North Avenue. In either case, get off at the intersection of North Avenue and Hilton Parkway. You will know that your stop is coming when the bus climbs past Poplar Grove, Longwood, and Rosedale streets.

From the corner of North Avenue and Hilton Parkway, walk south (or downhill) next to Hilton Parkway 0.2 mile to Morris Road on the right.

AUTOMOBILE: Gwynns Falls Park is located in west Baltimore immediately west of Hilton Parkway. The walk described here starts 0.2 mile south of the intersection of Hilton Parkway and North Avenue. However, the city's road planners propose to block access to Winterbourne Road and Morris Road from Hilton Parkway (see the map). If this is done, a new park entrance will be built off North Avenue just west of the intersection with Hilton Parkway.

From downtown Baltimore, take Route 40 west. After passing Western Cemetery on the left and crossing the bridge over the Gwynns Falls Valley, turn right immediately onto Hilton Parkway northbound. Follow the parkway north 0.8 mile; prepare to make a left turn. Immediately after passing an intersection with Morris Road on the left, turn left onto Winterbourne Road, where there is a parking area on the right side of the road just inside the gate. If Winterbourne Road has been closed, continue to North Avenue and turn left. Look for a new park entrance on the left.

Another approach is from North Avenue. Follow North Avenue west to the intersection with Hilton Parkway one block beyond the intersection with Ellamont Street. Turn left onto Hilton Parkway and follow it downhill 0.2 mile, then turn right at the first opportunity onto Winterbourne Road, where there is a parking area on the right side of the road just inside the gate. If Winterbourne Road has been closed, look for a new park entrance off North Avenue just west of the intersection with Hilton Parkway.

Yet another approach is from Interstate 695 (the Beltway) west of Baltimore. From the Beltway, take exit 15A for Route 40 east toward Baltimore. Follow Route 40 east for about 3.5 miles, then exit onto Hilton Parkway northbound. Follow Hilton Parkway north 1.0 mile. Prepare to make a left turn. Immediately after passing an intersection with Morris Road on the left, turn left onto Winterbourne Road, where there is a parking area on the right side of the road just inside the gate. If Winterbourne Road has been closed, continue to North Avenue and turn left. Look for a new park entrance on the left.

WALK: From the parking area on Winterbourne Road just west of Hilton Parkway, head downhill 50 yards across the grass to the intersection of Hilton Parkway and Morris Road. Bear right and follow the shoulder of Morris Road downhill a few dozen yards, then fork right onto a broad path sloping gradually uphill. Obviously, these directions may be affected by the proposed road changes noted above, but it should still be easy to locate the path that starts at the foot of the hill next to Morris Road.

Follow the path up along the side of the hill and then around to the right away from Hilton Parkway. If the path is overgrown with weeds and encroaching brush, simply plow ahead. After your walk, call the park headquarters (396–0010) and request that the millrace path be cleared; the fact of the matter is that the park department is so understaffed that it is often unaware of maintenance problems unless they are pointed out by park users.

Continue on the millrace path as it winds along the side of Gwynns Falls Valley. Eventually, cross a narrow asphalt road. (You will return later by the road ascending from the left.) With the valley on your left, continue along the path that follows the contour of the hillside. The path ends at Windsor Mill Road.

At Windsor Mill Road, turn around and retrace your steps about 300 yards (to just about the last point where the Windsor Mill Road bridge is still visible behind you) then fork right downhill on a broad path. Descend to the bottomland next to Gwynns Falls. With the river toward your right, follow a rough, obscure, rutted track along the bottomland several dozen yards from the river's edge. If *the track is overgrown, simply forge ahead through the tall grass and weeds. (Call the park headquarters after your return to ask that the meadow path be mowed periodically.) Continue as the bottomland spreads out into a wide meadow. Follow the rough track as it curves gradually left through the meadow and along the edge of the woods. Continue on the rough, rutted track until the path joins an asphalt road, and there turn left.*

With the valley on your left, follow the asphalt road gradually uphill. Where the path that you followed earlier crosses the road, turn right. With the valley on your right, follow the path along the hillside and back to the starting point at Hilton Parkway.

Postscript: Wouldn't it be nice if each autumn, at the peak of the fall color, the city were to close Franklintown Road for a weekend and invite the public to turn out for walking, running, or bicycling along the length of Gwynns Falls and Leakin parks—about 5.0 miles round-trip? I would go even further and suggest that the road be closed every weekend between 10 AM and 4 PM. When you recall that the automobile roads at Avalon (Chapter 1) and Loch Raven (Chapter 12) are closed every weekend, and that in consequence those areas have become very popular with walkers, joggers, and bicyclists, it seems likely that closing Franklintown Road on well-publicized occasions or on a regular schedule would attract many users to Gwynns Falls and Leakin parks. The Park & Ride lot at the end of Interstate 70 could provide ample parking space, and a short footpath and footbridge could link the lot with the western end of Franklintown Road. At the eastern end of the parks, roadside parking could be permitted off Franklintown Road just east of Hilton Parkway, where there are large, flat areas of gravel that seem to serve no use (unless as a dumping ground for trash). Finally, for about 100 yards east of the intersection with Winans Way, Franklintown Road would have to remain open to provide access to a private residence, but the traffic going to and from one house over this short stretch of road would hardly disrupt things.

Call the public relations desk at the Department of Recreation and Parks (396–7901) to make your opinion known. Perhaps the city will experiment with the notion.

Finally, a group interested in Baltimore's big wilderness parks is the Friends of Gwynns Falls/Leakin Park, 4921 Windsor Mill Road, Baltimore, MD 21207. The Carrie Murray Center (396–0808) just east of Crimea is another good place to make your concern known.

20

LEAKIN PARK

Walking and ski touring—2.0 miles (3.2 kilometers). Tour Crimea, an imposing nineteenth-century estate that has been preserved (more or less) as a city park. A trail follows an arborway of Osage-orange trees, then descends along the side of a wooded valley overlooking Dead Run. Return along a broad lawn leading up to the stone mansion. The park is open daily from sunrise to sunset. Dogs must be leashed. Managed by the Baltimore City Department of Recreation and Parks (telephone 396–0010).

THIS WALK EXPLORES CRIMEA, the country estate developed with a trainload of rubles by Baltimore's rolling stock magnate, Thomas DeKay Winans. The massive, almost cubic stone mansion was built shortly before the Civil War to overlook the valley of Dead Run at the western edge of the city. Named for the Soviet Riviera, Crimea was Winans's dacha—his summer home and winter hunting lodge. His intown residence was Alexandroffsky, formerly located in a private walled park east of present-day Union Square and described in various accounts as "palatial," "magnificent," "exotic," and "fabulous." Two cast-iron lions that used to guard Alexandroffsky were removed when it was razed in 1927 and now stand near the feline cages at the zoo in Druid Hill Park. Crimea fared better than Alexandroffsky and is now a part of Leakin Park.

The story of Winans's Russianisms and his Russian millions starts with his father, Ross Winans, a prominent inventor in the early days of the Baltimore & Ohio Railroad. After traveling

abroad with a group of experts sent by the B&O to study the English railroad system in 1828, Ross Winans worked on the adaptation of English engines and rolling stock to the steep grades and tight curves of the new American railroads. He reduced the friction of railroad wheels by fusing them with the axle so that the entire assembly revolved as a unit, with the axle turning in grease-packed boxes. This arrangement, with some modifications, is still in use around the world. Winans put the flange of the wheels on the inside edge and invented the swivel wheel truck and coned wheels with beveled treads to help trains negotiate curves. He was the first to use horizontal pistons on his *Crab* locomotives, and in time he built increasingly powerful engines, such as the *Camel* and the *Mud Digger,* to pull the B&O over the Allegheny Mountains. In 1835 Ross Winans and a partner assumed management of the B&O locomotive and rolling stock shops at Mt. Clare under an arrangement allowing them to sell equipment to other lines, provided that the B&O had first call. Then, in 1844 Ross Winans left the B&O and set up his own shop, where he built the *Carroll of Carrollton,* a locomotive said to be so fast for its day that its potential speed could never be tested because the railbeds were not sufficiently straight or evenly graded for the engine to be fully opened.

All of which brings us to the Russians, who in the late 1830s were embarking on their own railroad program. Czar Nicholas I had ordered the construction of a line between St. Petersburg and Moscow. Two Russian engineers came to the United States in 1839 to study American railroads and rolling stock, and they eventually recommended to the Russian government that George W. Whistler, a civil engineer trained at West Point (and incidentally father of the artist James A. McNeill Whistler), be hired to superintend construction of the new Russian line. Major Whistler knew Ross Winans; he and Winans had served together on the B&O commission to England, and Whistler had helped survey the B&O route. Whistler thought highly of Winans's locomotives and abilities. At Whistler's suggestion, Ross Winans was offered a contract in 1842 to set up a shop in Rus-

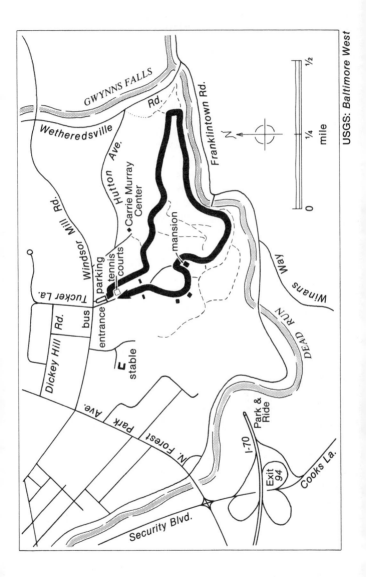

GWYNNS FALLS

Wetheredsville

Windsor Mill Rd.

Hutton Ave.

Rd.

Franklintown Rd.

Carrie Murray
Center

mansion

Tucker La.

parking

tennis
courts

entrance

bus

WINANS WAY

DEAD RUN

Dickey Hill Rd.

stable

N. Forest Park Ave.

Park &
Ride

I-70

Security Blvd.

Exit
94

Cooks La.

USGS: Baltimore West

N

0   ¼   ½
mile

sia to manufacture rolling stock in partnership with the Philadelphia firm of Harrison and Eastwick, which had been recommended by the two Russian engineers. Ross Winans declined on the grounds that he was too old, but he persuaded Whistler and the Russians to accept his two sons, Thomas and William, both of whom had worked under Ross in positions of responsibility.

In 1844 Harrison and Eastwick closed their Philadelphia locomotive shop and shipped their equipment to Alexandroffsky near St. Petersburg, where they were joined by the Winans brothers. A new shop was established and the partners embarked on an immensely lucrative contract to supply two hundred locomotives and seven thousand cars for the new Russian railroad, dubbed "the harnessed samovar" by the local populace. In 1850 the contract was expanded to include more equipment and ongoing maintenance. William Winans also designed and built iron bridges for the railroad, which was being laid out by Major Whistler. The Americans are said to have entertained lavishly, and judging from the estates that the Winans later built here and in England, they became accustomed to life in the grand style.

Thomas Winans returned home in 1854, three years after completion of the railroad. He brought with him a Russian wife of Italian and French ancestry and a fortune estimated at $2 million, which, of course, was a huge sum for those days. William Winans stayed in Europe and never returned to the United States. Nor did Major Whistler, who had encountered constant difficulties and delays in the construction of the railbed. Weakened by cholera, he died in 1849 before the line was completed.

Following his return to Baltimore, Thomas Winans designed and had constructed at his father's shop a streamlined "cigar ship." It was completely cylindrical and tapered to a point at each end like a submarine but was limited to surface travel. This design was intended to increase speed and economy by minimizing water resistance and top-heaviness in high winds and seas. Four of Ross Winans's locomotive engines powered a turbine-like wheel that completely circled the ship's waist, supposedly allowing the application of much more force than the midship paddlewheels of conventional steamers of the day. The ship was launched on October 6, 1858, at Winans Cove near the southern end of Light Street, but despite what newspaper accounts said were successful test runs nothing came of the design.

Another unusual venture of the Winans—in this case Ross Winans—was the repair at the outset of the Civil War of a steam-powered, self-propelled armored cannon—in short, a primitive tank. Invented and built by Charles S. Dickinson of Ohio, the gun was supposed to throw two hundred balls per minute from a revolving set of cupped arms, "just like so many hands throwing baseballs," according to William H. Weaver, a journalist and witness when the gun was tested at the Winans' factory. In less than a minute, the weapon demolished a brick wall buttressed with a pile of timbers three feet thick. An ardent and outspoken supporter of the Confederacy, Ross Winans attempted to send this gun to the South, but the weapon was intercepted by federal troops, who could not make it work. According to Mr. Weaver, a key piece of the mechanism had been removed before the gun was shipped and was to be sent only if the weapon reached its destination. In any case, Ross Winans was imprisoned briefly at Fort McHenry; after his release he was jailed again when he tried to send a shipload of arms to the Confederacy.

Unlike his father, the younger Winans was content to let the war take its own course. In the 1850s he had purchased a large tract of land in the vicinity of Gwynns Falls and Dead Run, and in 1860 he built the Crimea mansion, which shows a touch of Russia in its ornate carvings at the corners of the cornice and porch posts. Crimea was one of a number of spacious country estates developed in the Gwynns Falls area by wealthy Baltimore residents during the middle of the nineteenth century. The Crimea mansion was reached by a long entrance drive that climbed the hill from the Franklintown Road at the bottom of the valley. A semicircular masonry parapet halfway down the bluff was once decorated with a battery of dummy cannons, supposedly erected to resemble the Russian batteries at Balaklava, or according to another story, to deter passing Union troops from molesting the estate. A large undershot waterwheel that is still located near Franklintown Road pumped spring water to the house, and a gasworks manufactured gas for the principal residence. Near the main dwelling is the "Honeymoon House," which Winans built for his daughter when she married. The estate also has a caretaker's house, a large stone stable, and a vegetable cellar and ice house set into the slope at the bottom of the valley. The ground floor of the main house now serves as park headquarters, but there is some possibility that the mansion will be restored and put to other uses.

In 1866 Thomas Winans returned to Russia, where he served as president of the firm of Winans, Whistler, and Winans, managers of the St. Petersburg and Moscow Railroad under an eight-year contract with the Russian government. The Whistler in the firm's name was the son of the former superintendent and also the Winans' brother-in-law, having married Julia Winans while working in Ross Winans's Baltimore shops. After the management contract had run only two years, however, the Russian government took over the work and released the firm with the payment of a settlement of several million dollars. Thomas Winans returned home and divided his time between his houses, travel, and various charities until his death in 1878.

In 1941 the valley portion of the Crimea estate was purchased for a city park from Thomas Winans's heirs, and seven years later the city bought the balance. In both instances the purchase money was provided from the bequest of J. Wilson Leakin, an attorney who had died in 1922. Leakin had left several downtown properties to the city with the stipulation that the proceeds from their rental and eventual sale be used for the acquisition and improvement of a new city park. For years different neighborhood groups and municipal agencies wrangled about where the park should be located. Even after the first Crimea tract was purchased, Mayor Thomas D'Alesandro favored selling the property in 1947 because he thought it inaccessible, but instead the park was expanded in 1948 by the purchase of the Crimea grounds above the valley.

BUS: From downtown Baltimore, MTA bus #15 passes the Crimea entrance to Leakin Park at the intersection of Windsor Mill Road and Tucker Lane. You will know that your stop is coming when the bus turns off North Forest Park Avenue onto Dickey Hill Road and then turns uphill onto Tucker Lane. From the bus stop, cross Windsor Mill Road and enter the park between two stone posts surmounted by cast-iron eagles.

AUTOMOBILE: Leakin Park is located at Baltimore's western edge. The Crimea entrance to the park is on Windsor Mill Road directly opposite the intersection with Tucker Lane 0.3 mile east of the junction of Windsor Mill Road and North Forest Park Avenue.

From downtown Baltimore, follow Route 40 west past Hilton Parkway and Edmonson Village Shopping Center. After passing intersections with Old Frederick Road, Winans Way, and Nottingham Road, turn right onto Cooks Lane. Follow Cooks Lane 1.0 mile to an intersection (at a traffic light) with North Forest Park Avenue. Turn right onto North Forest Park Avenue and follow it uphill 0.5 mile to an intersection with Windsor Mill Road. Turn right and follow Windsor Mill Road 0.3 mile to the Crimea entrance on the right. Enter the park between stone posts surmounted by cast-iron eagles. Follow the entrance road only 100 yards, then turn left into the large parking lot.

Another approach is from Interstate 695 (the Beltway) west of Baltimore. From the Beltway, take exit 16 for Interstate 70, then fork east toward Park & Ride and "Downtown Buses." Follow Interstate 70 for 1.2 miles to exit 94 for Security Boulevard. From the bottom of the exit ramp, follow Security Boulevard only a few hundred yards. At the first traffic light, turn right onto North Forest Park Avenue.

Follow North Forest Park Avenue uphill 0.5 mile to an intersection with Windsor Mill Road. Turn right and follow Windsor Mill Road 0.3 mile to the Crimea entrance on the right. Enter the park between stone posts surmounted by cast-iron eagles. Follow the entrance road only 100 yards, then turn left into the large parking lot.

WALK: Start at the asphalt path connecting the parking lot and the tennis courts. Facing the tennis courts, turn left off the asphalt path and continue between two parallel hedges. Do not enter the woods; instead, bear right and pass behind the tennis courts. Continue with the woods on your left and a hedge and lawn on your right as the path becomes an arborway under the arched branches of Osage-orange trees. Follow the arborway path as it bends left, but then continue straight where a side trail veers left into the woods (toward the Carrie Murray Outdoor Education Center). With a hedge and a lawn on your right, continue straight downhill and into the woods.

Follow the path downhill through the woods. Pass a trail intersecting from the right. Cross a small masonry bridge with iron hoops for railings. Continue along the side of the valley of Dead Run, where the stream is sometimes visible downhill to the right. Follow the trail as it descends past immense tulip trees and obscure side trails.

Continue through the woods to a T-intersection and then turn right. Go 50 yards to another T-intersection in front of Dead Run, then turn right again. With the stream toward your left, continue through wooded bottomland. Pass a long stone wall on your left. Pass a bridge on your left and enter a broad lawn sloping uphill. Follow the lawn uphill and around to the right as the lawn narrows. Continue along a rolling swath of lawn to the Crimea mansion.

From the driveway in front of the mansion—and with your back toward the front door—turn left and follow the looping driveway clockwise past the honeymoon cottage and a garage. Be alert for cars. Follow the edge of the road to the parking lot.

21

HERRING RUN

*Walking—up to 3.0 miles (4.8 kilometers). Explore a waste-
land of weeds, low brush, woods, and rubbish along both
banks of Herring Run, currently awaiting park development.
What would you do if you were assigned the task of designing
a park here? A path of sorts extends along the west bank, but
the east bank is terra incognita. The "park" is open daily
from sunrise to sunset. Dogs must be leashed. Managed by the
Baltimore City Department of Recreation and Parks (telephone 396–8526).*

ALTHOUGH OWNED by Baltimore City and assigned to the
Department of Recreation and Parks, the banks of Herring Run
between Sinclair Lane and Pulaski Highway are as yet largely
undeveloped for park purposes, nor are there any proposals for
improvement of the area in the near future. Most of the west
bank is weedy meadows and willow thickets crisscrossed by
trailbike paths. The mounded east bank is recent landfill. Herring Run itself, which carries stormwater runoff from the
northeast sector of the city and from parts of Baltimore County,
is a sort of urban arroyo of gravel bars and gabions—that is,
crushed rock encased in large wire cages along the banks
to retard erosion. Nonetheless, as Lancelot Brown, the
eighteenth-century landscape architect, would have said, this
unprepossessing wasteland "has capabilities"—a phrase
Brown used so often that he became known as Capability
Brown.

Now it is your turn to exercise your capacity for park design. If you have taken some of the other walks described in this book, you have had a chance to form your own opinion about what makes a successful park. You undoubtedly have seen (and occasionally have smelled and heard) some of the problems of gross misuse, under- and overuse, and conflicting use from which parks suffer. This walk has been included here despite its crudeness so that you can examine a stretch of land currently in limbo and determine what you would recommend, if you were the city's planning consultant.

Upstream from Sinclair Lane, Herring Run has already been developed into Baltimore's longest linear park, stretching from Baltimore County south past Mount Pleasant Golf Course, Morgan State, and Lake Montebello. So, if you are repelled by the section of Herring Run explored by this walk, you can recover your spirits by following the winding asphalt path along either bank of the stream between Harford and Belair roads in what is currently one of Herring Run Park's nicer sections. Or perhaps you will like the wasteland described here (as I do) and be attracted by its potential for park development.

In Baltimore, the impetus to create or refurbish a park usually comes from neighborhood groups or a coalition of such groups. Herring Run enjoys staunch support from several groups, including the Friends of Northeast Parks and Streams, whose president in 1987 was Councilman Jody Landers. If such a group were to express a persistent interest in the area south of Sinclair Lane, it is likely that the city would eventually arrange for the preparation of a park development plan to explore the issue.

Obviously, one of the first steps taken by park planners is an inspection of the area to determine the basic terrain with which they must work, as well as those less permanent features of the landscape that are worth preserving and enhancing. In recent years standard land planning practice has included a site inventory and analysis of such factors as topography, slopes, geology, soils, stream patterns and quality, vegetation and forest types, animal life, historic sites, and existing facilities, al-

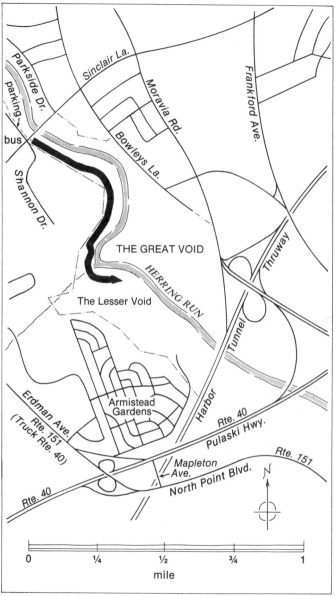

USGS: *Baltimore East*

though it is sometimes difficult to determine afterwards what practical use has been made of this mass of information. Planners must also note problems that need to be remedied, such as eyesores that should be screened with trees and shrubs. Also, access to the park must be provided from major roads and surrounding residential areas as well as between separate areas of the park. Finally, planners should be cognizant of concurrent development plans for nearby sites that might enhance or conflict with the contemplated park. For example, part of the city's property along Bosley Lane east of Herring Run might be put to use as a transfer station for the consolidation and shipping of trash.

Soil (or more accurately rubbish) is a critical factor at Herring Run. Much of the land along the stream between Sinclair Lane and Pulaski Highway is underlain by unburned refuse that will continue to settle for many years. The futility of building playing fields on this foundation of trash is demonstrated by just such an attempt near Armistead Gardens on the west bank by the Harbor Tunnel Thruway, where large hollows have developed in the fields since they were graded in 1978.

After becoming familiar with the area, the planners then meet with the residents of nearby neighborhoods to determine their general concerns and recommendations as well as their specific requests for different kinds of facilities, from tennis courts to tot lots. Despite preconceptions about what might be suitable, the planners quickly learn that most residents want facilities that will provide conveniences and amenities for their own use or will improve the tone of the neighborhood but attract as few outsiders as possible. Residents bordering the park understandably expect that facilities that attract crowds—even something as innocuous as a bicycle path—be located deep within the park at a distance from their homes or not built at all. For example, in 1984 the city contemplated building an ice rink in upper Herring Run Park, but local residents objected and the rink was put elsewhere. In most instances, however, a consensus is gradually reached through a series of public meetings, where objections and proposed solutions are reviewed.

In addition to site characteristics and neighborhood preferences, another conspicuous design constraint is development cost. Roads, structures, and extensive regrading of the surface are particularly expensive. In 1978, the city spent $500,000 for improvements on the west bank of Herring Run just north of the Harbor Tunnel Thruway. The funds paid for a drainage system, several football and baseball fields, two tennis courts, picnic tables, toilets, a playground, a parking lot, and an access road. An inspection of the improvements shows that relative to the whole area between Sinclair Lane and Pulaski Highway, the money did not go very far. (As noted before, the project was also a complete waste because of subsequent settlement of the land.)

Upkeep is yet another consideration. Maintenance is funded largely by the city's ordinary tax revenues and accordingly is in very short supply. A park should require a minimum of maintenance while continuing to be attractive and to serve the use for which it was intended. In addition to ordinary wear and tear, planners must anticipate the indefatigable zeal of vandals to deface, smash, raze, and obliterate anything of less than Gibraltar-like permanence. For example, the park toilets built in 1978—indeed, the very structures housing the toilets—have already been destroyed by vandals who have knocked man-sized holes through the concrete-block walls, rather as though these lavatories were bank vaults loaded with gold. Even something as ordinary as a sign is immediately attacked. Upstream from Sinclair Lane, a series of signs and exercise stations for jogging and calisthenics was installed in 1978 along the bicycle path at a cost of $4000 (donated by the Sun Life Insurance Company of America), but the signs have largely been obliterated by vandals, as was a nature trail for the blind built at the McKeldin Area of the Patapsco Valley State Park. Another form of abuse that plagues our parks is the dumping of trash.

Finally, from the often conflicting constraints dictated by the character of the site, the desires of different groups, and budgetary and maintenance considerations, planners must establish priorities and develop a design that makes the most of the opportunities presented. Not surprisingly, because of the emphasis on consensus and compromise in park planning, the result is sometimes a discouraging blandness that is exemplified by the stretch of Herring Run immediately north of Sinclair Lane. Any ideas for the area to the south?

BUS: From downtown Baltimore, take the MTA Cedonia bus (#5) via Baltimore, Gay, Preston, and Federal streets to Herring Run. Get off at Shannon Drive or Parkside Way, where Sinclair Lane crosses Herring Run. You will know that your stop is coming when the bus turns right from Clareway onto Sinclair Lane.

AUTOMOBILE: The section of Herring Run explored by this walk is located in east Baltimore. The walk starts where Sinclair Lane crosses Herring Run, 0.7 mile east of the intersection of Sinclair Lane and Erdman Avenue.

From downtown Baltimore, follow Route 40 east (Orleans Street, then Pulaski Highway). After passing under three railroad bridges and going under the Erdman Avenue bridge, turn right onto Mapletown Avenue at a traffic light, then turn right again onto Erdman Avenue (Route 151). Follow Erdman Avenue 1.4 miles, then turn right onto Sinclair Lane. Follow Sinclair Lane 0.7 mile to a crossroads with Shannon Drive at a traffic light, and there turn left and park on the side of Shannon Drive.

Another approach is from Interstate 695 (the Beltway) east of Baltimore. Take exit 35W (which may be changed to 35A) for Route 40 west toward Baltimore. Follow Route 40 west about 4.0 miles, then exit onto Route 151 and Truck Route 40 (Erdman Avenue) west. Follow Erdman Avenue 1.2 miles, then turn right onto Sinclair Lane. Follow Sinclair Lane 0.7 mile to a crossroads with Shannon Drive at a traffic light, and there turn left and park on the side of Shannon Drive.

WALK: With the stream valley on your left, follow an asphalt bicycle path downstream from the corner of Sinclair Lane and Shannon Drive. The bicycle path lies about 50 yards from the stream, so you may prefer to walk along the river's edge. Where the bicycle path ends, continue on a dirt track along the river. Ford a small stream (but only if the water is not more than ankle deep) and continue with Herring Run on your left.

To explore the east bank of Herring Run, return to Sinclair Lane, cross the bridge, then walk downstream as you did on the west bank.

BIBLIOGRAPHY

The numbers in parentheses at the end of the citations refer to the chapters in this book that are based on the cited material.

Abbott, Collamer L. "Isaac Tyson, Jr., Pioneer Mining Engineer and Metallurgist." *Maryland Historical Magazine.* March, 1965. (6)

The Allen Organization. *Study for a Proposed Gunpowder River Valley Park System.* Maryland State Planning Commission, 1958. (8)

Allen, Paul. *Conservation Easements.* Baltimore: Maryland Environmental Trust, 1977. (7)

Andrews, Matthew Page. *History of Maryland: Province and State.* Garden City, N Y: Doubleday, Doran & Company, 1929. (17)

Andrews, Matthew Page. *Tercentenary History of Maryland.* Chicago: S.T. Clarke Publishing Company, 1925. (17)

Baltimore Region Water Quality Management Plan—Summary: Clean Enough for Fishing and Swimming? Baltimore: Regional Planning Council, 1979. (13)

Baylin, Lee. "Md. Still Seeking to Buy Park Lands 13 Years Later." *The Evening Sun.* July 22, 1971. (8)

Bee, Avery M. "Wool-Weaving Dickeys Have a 100-Year Record," *The Sun.* March 27, 1938. (3)

Borror, Donald J. *Common Bird Songs.* New York: Dover Publications, Inc., 1967. (11)

Brockman, C. Frank. *Trees of North America.* New York: Golden Press, 1968. (18)

Carson, Larry. "State Moving to Buy Houses in Park." *The Evening Sun.* March 31, 1978. (8)

"City To Purchase Rest of Leakin Park Tract." *The Evening Sun.* April 8, 1947. (20)

Collins, Joan. "Daniels—History of a Lost River Valley," *Ellicott City Heritage.* September, 1979. (4)

Corbett, Edward S. "Water Resources in the Urban Forest Environment." In *Proceedings of the National Urban Forestry Conference, Washington, DC November, 1978; ESF Publication 80–003, 1980.* (13)

Corbett, Edward S., and Warren Spencer. "*Effects of Management Practices on Water Quality and Quantity; Baltimore, Maryland, Municipal Watersheds.*" In *Municipal Watershed Management Symposium Proceedings, USDA Forest Service General Technical Report NE–13.* (13)

"*Crimea Picked Finally for Leakin Park.*" *The Sun.* June 8, 1940. (20)

Daniel, Mann, Johnson & Mendenhall. *Master Development Plan: Patapsco State Park.* Annapolis: Maryland Department of Forests and Parks, 1971. (5)

"A Day at the Crimea." *The Sunday Herald.* April 22, 1894. (20)

"Dickey Mill Now Industrial Park." *The News American.* September 16, 1973. (3)

Dilts, James D. "Can State Clean Up Polluted Patapsco?" *The Sun.* August 20, 1967. (5)

Dilts, James D. "Death Of A Town," *The Sun.* May 12, 1968. (4)

Dunn, Linda. "Old Mill Houses of Daniels to Come Tumbling Down." *The Sun.* May 23, 1967. (4)

Hugh Ely v. David Steward and J.J. Speed, Trustees, 2 Md. 408 (1852). (4)

The Elysville Manufacturing Company v. The Okisko Company, 5 Md. 152 (1853). (4)

The Elysville Manufacturing Company v. The Okisko Company et al., 1 Md. ch. 392 (1849). (4)

Evans, Charles W., ed. *Biographical and Historical Accounts of the Fox, Ellicott, and Evans Families.* Buffalo: Baker, Jones & Co., 1882. (1, 3, 4)

Final Environmental Statement. Report No. FHWA-MD-EIS–72–10-
  D-F. U.S. Department of Transportation, Federal Highway Admin-
  istration; Maryland Department of Transportation, State Highway
  Administration, 1975. (19)

"Fort Howard Opens Park Doors." *The Dundalk Times.* September
  18, 1975. (17)

"Fort Howard Water Plan Set," *The Sun.* April 20, 1977. (17)

Garrels, Robert M. *A Textbook of Geology.* New York: Harper &
  Brothers, 1951. (14, 15)

Gilbert, Kelly. "City Eyes Giving Bridges to State." *The Evening
  Sun.* March 23, 1981. (19)

Gottschalk, L.C. *Report on the Reconnaissance Sedimentation Surveys of Loch Raven and Prettyboy Reservoirs, Baltimore, Maryland.* Washington, D.C.: U. S. Department of Agriculture, Soil
  Conservation Service, 1943. (8)

Greene, Suzanne Ellery. *An Illustrated History: Baltimore.* Woodland
  Hills, Calif.: Windsor Publications, Inc., 1980. (6)

Gunpowder Falls State Park: Master Plan. Annapolis: Department of
  Natural Resources, 1983. (8)

Hartley, Brent A. "Current Management Practices on the Baltimore
  Municipal Watersheds." In *Municipal Watershed Management
  Symposium Proceedings,* USDA Forest Service General Technical
  Report NE–13, 1975. (12, 13)

Hartley, Brent A., and Warren G. Spencer. "Management Problems
  and Techniques on a City Watershed." Paper presented at National
  Urban Forestry Conference, Washington, D.C., November, 1978.
  (12, 13)

Hay, Jacob. "Crimea, The Mansion Rubles Built, Opens Doors to All
  of Baltimore." *The Sun.* June 14, 1948. (20)

Henry, Frank. "City Playground—37 Miles Long." *The Sun.* November 5, 1950. (5)

Henry, Frank. "Patapsco State Park—Maryland's Second Biggest
  Park." *The Sun Magazine.* August 14, 1956. (5)

Hines, Bob. *Ducks at a Distance.* Ottawa: Canadian Wildlife Service,
  1965. (11)

Holland, Celia M. *Ellicott City, Maryland: Mill Town, U.S.A.* Chicago: Adams Press, 1970. (3)

"Home of Mrs. Bruce Cotton, Cylburn will be Public Park." *The Sun.* September 29, 1942. (18)

Horton, Tom. "Environmental Groups Work to Remove Cap on Revenue for Project Open Space." *The Sun.* October 19, 1986. (8)

Hughes, T. Lee. "V.O.L.P.E. a Road Block." *The News American.* August 22, 1971. (19)

"Jackson Calls Group to Act on Leakin Bequest." *The Evening Sun.* July 1, 1938. (20)

James, Alfred R. "Sidelights on the Founding of the Baltimore & Ohio Railroad." *Maryland Historical Magazine.* December 1953.(3)

Joynes, J. William. "Company Town." *The News American,* December 9, 1956. (4)

Keene, John C. *Untaxing Open Space.* Washington, D.C.: Council on Environmental Quality, 1970. (7)

Klein, Richard D. *An Integrated Watershed Management Policy for Baltimore County, Maryland.* Annapolis: Department of Natural Resources, 1980. (13)

Kreh, Charles F. "Saw Ellicott City Flood and Tells Grim Story of Awful Havoc There." *The Sun.* February 15, 1920. (1)

Levin, Alexandra Lee. "A Russian Railroad Made the Winans Family Rich." *The Sun Magazine.* October 10, 1976. (20)

Marye, William B. "A Commentary on Certain Words and Expressions Used in Maryland." *Maryland Historical Magazine.* June, 1951. (9)

Marye, William B. "Place Names of Baltimore and Harford Counties." *Maryland Historical Magazine.* September, 1958. (16)

Maryland Geological Survey: Baltimore County. Baltimore: Johns Hopkins Press, 1929. (6, 14, 15)

McGrain, John W. *Grist Mills in Baltimore County, Maryland.* Towson, Md.: Baltimore County Public Library, 1980. (2, 3)

McGrain, John W. "Historical Aspects of Lake Roland. *Maryland Historical Magazine.* September, 1979. (10, 11, 13)

McGrain, John W. *The Molinography of Maryland: A Tabulation of Mills, Furnaces, and Primitive Industries.* Towson, Maryland, 1968. Revised and expanded, 1976. (1, 2, 3, 4, 11, 16)

McGrain, John W. *Oella—Its Thread of History.* Oella, Md.: Oella Community Improvement Association, 1976. (3)

McGrain, John W. *From Pig Iron to Cotton Duck*. Towson, Md.: Baltimore County Public Library, 1985. (1, 3, 7, 14, 16)

McKerrow, Stephen. "Daniels Mill is Declared a National Historic Site." *The Evening Sun*. May 14, 1973. (4)

Morison, Samuel Eliot. *The Oxford History of the American People*. New York: Oxford University Press, 1965. (17)

Movement Against Destruction v. Volpe, 361 F. Supp. 1360 (D. Md. 1973). (19)

Nielsen, Craig A. "Preservation of Maryland Farmland: A Current Assessment." *University of Baltimore Law Review*. Vol. 8, No. 3, 1979. (7)

Northern Baltimore County Citizens Committee. *Hereford Area Plan: Gunpowder State Park*. 1979. (8)

Northern Central Railroad Trail, Gunpowder Falls State Park: Draft Master Plan. Annapolis: Department of Natural Resources, 1987. (10)

"Outrages Upon the Corporate Rights of Baltimore." *Baltimore Patriot*. April, 1850. (10)

"Over $1,800,000 Flood Damage in Park; River Changes Course; Public Warned About Danger." *The Catonsville Times*. July 20, 1972. (1)

Overview Statement for Interstate 70N and Interstate 170 in West Baltimore, Baltimore, Maryland. U.S. Department of Transportation, Federal Highway Administration; Maryland Department of Transportation, State Highway Administration, 1975. (19)

"Park Expansion Imperils 4 Homes." *The News American*. February 28, 1979. (8)

"Park Section is Dedicated." *The Sun*. June 17, 1957. (5)

"Patapsco Courses 50 Miles from Pond to Port." *The Evening Sun*. November 2, 1976. (5)

Patapsco Valley State Park: Concept Plan. Annapolis: Department of Natural Resources, 1976. (5)

Patapsco Valley State Park: Master Plan. Annapolis: Department of Natural Resources, 1981. (5)

"Patapsco's Beauty to be Preserved." *The News American*. June 6, 1912. (5)

Pearre, Nancy C., and Allen V. Heyl. *Chromite and Other Mineral*

Deposits in Serpentine Rocks of the Piedmont Upland, Maryland, Pennsylvania, and Delaware. Geological Survey Bulletin 1082-K. Washington, D.C.: Government Printing Office, 1960. (6)

Peterson, Roger Tory. *How to Know the Birds.* New York: Mentor Books, 1949. (11)

Petrides, George A. *A Field Guide to Trees and Shrubs.* Boston: Houghton Mifflin Company, 1958. (18)

Phieffer, C. Boyd. "Soldiers Delight." *The News American.* March 17, 1968. (6)

Phillips, Thomas L. "Orange Grove as a Busy Mill Village." *The Sun Magazine.* June 25, 1967. (2)

Phillips, Thomas L. *The Orange Grove Story.* Washington, D.C., 1972. (2)

Platt, Rutherford. *American Trees, A Book of Discovery.* New York: Dodd, Mead, & Company, 1952. (18)

Program Open Space—Ten Year Report: 1969–1979. Annapolis: Department of Natural Resources, 1980. (8)

Report of the Mayor's Advisory Committee on Herring Run to the Mayor and City Council of Baltimore City. 1977–1978. (21)

Robbins, Chandler S., Bertel Bruun, and Herbert S. Zim. *Birds of North America.* New York: Golden Press, 1966 (11)

Robbins, Michael W. *Maryland's Iron Industry During the Revolutionary War Era.* Annapolis: Maryland Bicentennial Committee, 1973. (16)

Scarupa, Henry. "A Ghost Town With a Band." *The Sun Magazine.* October 14, 1973. (16)

Scharf, Thomas J. *The Chronicles of Baltimore.* Baltimore: Turnbull Brothers, 1874. (17)

"$180,000 Set For Leakin Park Use." *The Evening Sun.* March 27, 1947. (20)

"Shrinking Maryland Farmland." *The Sun.* February 15, 1981. (7)

Siegel, Eric. "Saving Open Land." *The Sun Magazine.* July 6, 1980. (7)

Stump, William. "The Man Behind the Iron Horse." *The Sun Magazine.* February 24, 1952. (20)

Stump, William. "Street Signs: Cylburn Avenue." *The Sun Magazine.* July 18, 1954. (18)

Tuemmler, Fred W., and Associates. *Master Development Plan: Gun-*

powder *River Valley State Park.* College Park, Md.: 1967. (8)

Urban Design Concept Associates. *Corridor Development: Baltimore Interstate Highway System 3-A/Segment 9.* 1970. (19)

Vokes, Harold E., and Jonathan Edwards. *Maryland Geological Survey.* Baltimore, 1974. (6, 14, 15)

Walsh, Jean. "This Week Marks a Century Since the Great Flood" *The Catonsville Times.* July 25, 1968. (1)

Walsh, Richard, and William Lloyd Fox, eds. *Maryland, A History: 1632–1974.* Baltimore: Maryland Historical Society, 1974. (3, 17)

Ward v. Ackroyd, 344 F. Supp. 1202 (D. Md. 1972). (19)

Ward v. Mayor and City Council of Baltimore, 267 Md. 576, 298 A.2d 382 (1973). (19)

Warfield, J.D. *The Founders of Anne Arundel and Howard Counties, Maryland.* Baltimore: Kohn & Pollock, 1905. (3)

Joseph White and Thomas White v. The Okisko Company, et al., 3 Md. ch. 214 (1852). (4)

Whyte, William H. *The Last Landscape.* Garden City, N.Y.: Doubleday & Company, Inc., 1968. (7)

"Will the East-West Highway Ever Get Built?" *The News American.* April 8, 1974. (19)

"Winans Steam Gun Mystery is Solved." *The News American.* April 12, 1911. (20)

"The Winans Steamer." *Harper's Weekly.* October 23, 1858. (20)